ETHNOGRAPHIC FILM

D1019322

ETHNOGRAPHIC FILM

Revised Edition

BY KARL G. HEIDER

UNIVERSITY OF TEXAS PRESS

Austin

Copyright © 1976, 2006 by the University of Texas Press
All rights reserved
Printed in the United States of America
Third paperback printing, 2011

Requests for permission to reproduce material from this work
should be sent to:
Permissions
University of Texas Press
P.O. Box 7819
Austin, TX 78713-7819
www.utexas.edu/utpress/about/bpermission.html

∞ The paper used in this book meets the minimum requirements of
ANSI/NISO Z39.48-1992 (R1997) (Permanence of Paper).

LIBRARY OF CONGRESS CATALOGING-IN-PUBLICATION DATA

Heider, Karl G., 1935–
Ethnographic film / by Karl G. Heider.—Rev. ed.
    p.   cm.
Includes bibliographical references and index.
ISBN 978-0-292-71458-8 (pbk. : alk. paper)
    1. Motion pictures in ethnology.   2. Motion pictures in
ethnology—Study and teaching.   I. Title.
    GN347.H44   2006
    305.8—dc22   2006019479

To Robert Gardner
And to the memory of
Jean Rouch
John Marshall
Timothy Asch

CONTENTS

PREFACE

W hat is "ethnographic film"? The term itself seems to embody an inherent tension or conflict between two ways of seeing and understanding, two strategies for bringing order to (or imposing order on) experience: the scientific and the aesthetic. The evolution of ethnographic filmmaking has been a continuous process attempting to reconcile this tension, to achieve a fertile synthesis. Ideally, ethnographic films unite the art and skills of the filmmaker with the trained intellect and insights of the ethnographer. This book examines the implications and the opportunities of such a collaboration; its argument rests on the fundamental assumption that film can be an important medium for the expression of the ethnographic enterprise. What is involved, though, is more demanding than a mere mechanical joining of cinematography and ethnography. There must be interpenetration of disciplines: cinematographers must accept the scientific demands of ethnography; ethnographers must adapt their expressions to the expanded visual potential of film and video. Filmmakers must think ethnographically, or scientifically; ethnographers must think cinematographically, or visually. There are great challenges on both sides, and the burgeoning vitality of ethnographic film testifies to the rewards as these challenges are met.

This book is written for people in film, for people in anthropology, and for the increasing number of people who are concerned with both, such as teachers who use these films in their classrooms. Most of it is an attempt to develop a systematic way of thinking about ethnographic film, and in particular about the "ethnographicness" of film. The issues that it treats are very close to the concerns of primatologists, sociologists, geographers, and psychologists. These neighboring specialists will have little trouble translating it into their own idiom to deal with their own interests.

We have to be very careful when talking of the differences between film and ethnography. We will find enough real problems without fostering an unnecessary rivalry. Three important points should be brought up immediately.

First, the simple opposition of scientific ethnography versus artistic cinematography is misleading. Film has its share of science, both in the technology of filmmaking itself and, on another level, in the theorizing about film that has been going on for decades. On the other side, ethnography is a most impure science whose research often is carried out by a relatively private field experience. As we think about the natures of film and ethnography in the next chapters, each will shed new and interesting light on the other.

The second major point is that when the demands of ethnography and film seem to conflict and we choose to fulfill the ethnographic demands in order to have a more ethnographic film, the result will probably turn out to be a better film even by cinematographic standards. The ethnographic approach will seem strange at first in some respects to many filmmakers. But I hope to demonstrate that, in the long run, better ethnography will make for better cinematography. And third, although we are thinking about ethnographic film, and developing ways to judge ethnographicness in film, this does not imply any moral superiority for one sort of film over another. There are many worthy sorts of films. This book is about one sort, namely, ethnographic film. Likewise, there are many valid ways to look at human behavior. This book is about one way, namely, ethnography. In short, I am not presuming to make over the world film industry along the lines of ethnographic precepts; but at the same time I resist the careless expropriation of the term *ethnographic* to cover any film about people.

A word of explanation about terminology: I use "ethnography" and "anthropology" more or less interchangeably here. Ethnographers are anthropologists who study human behavior. They call themselves ethnographers, ethnologists, social anthropologists, cultural anthropologists, anthropologists, social scientists, or scientists, depending on the context and the audience. Some of them care very deeply about these labels and spend a lot of energy on label clarification. I don't, but I apologize for any offense caused.

A second terminological note: even though more and more of these products are shot, edited, and distributed on videotape or DVDs, I am using the old term "ethnographic film" to include film, tape, and disc. For some sorts of discussions it is necessary to distinguish among the various media. But for the purpose of this book, the single phrase "ethnographic film" will do. And in fact, these days we are often not told if a particular product originated on celluloid or tape, in analog or digital form. So, for "film," despite an occasional infelicitous phrasing, please understand "film or videotape or disc."

There are two rather different uses of film in anthropology. One is the subject of this book, that is, finished films that have been made for public showing and that present some sort of ethnographic understanding. But anthropologists also use the movie camera and the videotape recorder to make visual records of human behavior that may be analyzed in real time or may be subjected to detailed, micro-, or slow-motion analysis. These raw data are footage or film, but they are not films. After the analysis has been made, the footage may be edited into a film for public presentation of the results of the analysis, just as raw material is often incorporated into scientific papers and monographs. Gregory Bateson's footage from Bali in the 1930s, edited into film by Margaret Mead a decade later, and Ray L. Birdwhistell's film *Microcultural Incidents in Ten Zoos* are two of the few examples of footage that has served both functions. The use of film (and videotape) to make visual records for behavioral analysis is a powerful tool in anthropological research. However, this still lags far behind the development of ethnographic film. But see, for example, books by Banks and Morphy (1977), Pink (2001), and Pink et al. (2004).

This book has three characteristics that are not universally admired: it is polemic, it is repetitive, and it speaks in different tongues to different audiences. It might help matters to explain why I feel that each is a useful strategy. We will never have *the* definitive book on ethnographic film. The whole multifaceted subject is very much in a state of flux, and we do need strong statements that organize some of the chaos and push ahead the thinking about ethnographic film. That is what I tried to do in the first edition, what many others have also tried to do, and what I continue in this new edition. I do not see this book as definitive. But it does mean to continue the debate(s) about ethnographic film.

The repetition comes from a strategy of crisscrossing exposition. The subject of ethnographic film has so many facets that it must be approached from many different directions in order to be at all exhaustive. The problem simply does not lend itself to a logical chain exposition. Thus, the same principle may be treated in one way in the theoretical chapter 1, another way in the historical chapter 2, yet another way in chapter 3, which is on attributes, and then restated in reference to ethnographic filmmakers (chapter 4) and to teachers (chapter 5). The readers' indulgence for such repetition is begged on the grounds that each reappearance will add to the development of the ideas.

Since the first edition of this book in 1976, many others have appeared on the subject (e.g., Stoller 1992, Loizos 1993, Morris 1994, MacDougall 1998, Ruby 2000, Grimshaw 2001, and El Guindi 2004, to mention just a few). We have all differed on points large and small. But in this second edition, rather than trying to concur, refute, or reconcile in detail, I have refined and updated the information and the perspectives of the first edition.

And finally, I am hoping that the various audiences of anthropologists, filmmakers, schoolteachers, and interested others can all be comfortable between the covers of a single book. No one group will want to read every page. But each audience has some concerns in common with each other audience, and in any case it is often good to know what is being said to others.

This is a fairly personal book in the sense that I draw heavily on my own experience in studying the Grand Valley Dani of Irian Jaya, Indonesia (the province has also been called Netherlands New Guinea, West New Guinea, Irian Barat, and Papua). I spent nearly three years doing research among the Dani on four trips between 1961 and 1970 (and brief visits in 1988 and 1995). I have described the Dani in an ethnographic monograph (*The Dugum Dani,* 1970), a case study (*Grand Valley Dani,* 1997), and numerous papers, as well as through two short films (*Dani Sweet Potatoes* and *Dani Houses*), and, during my first months with the Dani, I collaborated with Robert Gardner as he made the film *Dead Birds.* More recently I have spent another three years studying emotion and folk psychology with the Minangkabau of West Sumatra. I used video in my research but have not yet made an ethnographic film about the Minangkabau. I could never understand my own professors who had done original research but who, from some misguided sense of modesty perhaps, taught only from other people's data and refused to discuss their fieldwork. My own experience as an ethnographer as well as an ethnographic filmmaker is so directly pertinent to a book on ethnographic film that I can hardly pretend noninvolvement. Also, I know my own ethnography and my own films better than I do anyone else's. And I can criticize them with impunity.

Should a book on ethnographic film include photographs or not? When writing the first edition, I finally decided against it. It could have had photographs of the various filmmakers, cameras at hand, standing on location: interesting, but not essential. It could have "production stills" of the sort displayed outside movie theaters. These are still shots that were taken during the filming, but they rarely show scenes that are actually in the film itself. Or it could have photographs printed directly from frames in the film, but necessarily of poor technical quality by the time they reached the printed page. However, the real problem with still photographs in a book like this is that we are concerned with the problems that emerge from trying to make sense out of long sequences of moving pictures, while a still photograph is, after all, still. Ideally there would be a short film to illustrate the principles discussed here. Thirty years later I still include no photographs, but I have no doubt that in another thirty years works like this will be able to include film clips along with the text.

Inevitably a book such as this one puts great demands on the readers' imagination because of the constant reference to scenes from various ethnographic films. I have tried to keep the references limited to the films that are best known and most widely available. (The film catalog in the appendix will be of help here.) And I have tried to make the references explicit enough that even readers who cannot view the films will be able to visualize the scenes.

ACKNOWLEDGMENTS

During the last decades I have shamelessly lifted ideas about ethnographic film from countless sources. I can only begin to do justice in acknowledging those who have contributed in one way or another to this book.

First and foremost, I am indebted to Robert Gardner, who introduced me to ethnographic film and invited me to accompany him to New Guinea. Like so many others, I have benefited tremendously from his time, energy, and insights, all most generously given.

Teaching a course jointly with someone else can be a strenuous educational experience for all concerned, and I have learned much from interactions with my many coteachers in ethnographic film courses: Robert Gardner (Harvard, 1966); Henry Breitrose (Stanford, 1972); Jay Ruby, Sol Worth, and Carroll Williams (Summer Institute for Visual Anthropology, 1972); Richard Hawkins and John Bohm (University of California, Los Angeles, 1973–1974); and John Heider (University of California, Berkeley, Extension, 1974). Others whose influence has been especially important are Timothy Asch, Donald Rundstrom, Ronald Rundstrom, Alan Lomax, and the participants in the Summer Institute for Visual Anthropology in Santa Fe, 1972. And it was Carroll Williams who generously gave me the use of his experience and his lab in Santa Fe to finish my own two Dani films.

For their comments on the first edition, I am particularly grateful to Ernest Callenbach, Bambi Schieffelin, Robert Gardner, Paul Ekman, Henry Breitrose, and Cameron Macauley.

The first edition of this book was finished during the fall of 1975, when I was a Fellow at the Center for Advanced Study in the Behavioral Sciences in Stanford, California. My warm thanks go to that most humane of institutions.

This second edition is being written as I take a brief break to serve in the University of South Carolina administration. My thanks go to Provost Mark P. Becker and to all the others in the Provost's Office who have encouraged me to steal precious moments to work on this and other projects. Also thanks to my colleagues in the USC Film Studies Program, particularly Ina Hark, Dan Streible, Laura Kissell, and Karla Berry. So many other students and colleagues at home and abroad have helped me to think about ethnographic film that I cannot name them all, but at least I should mention Tim Asch, Tom and Pam Blakely, Carol Hermer (who stepped in to help with the eighth edition of *Films for Anthropological Teaching*), Charles and Marjorie Goodwin, James Hoesterey, and, most recently, Kim Cavanagh, Bridget McDonnell, Meredith Badinelli, and Paul Heider (who helped with computer problems).

Ethnographic film as a field is unique. I know of no other field where people care so deeply and differ so bitterly. It does make things exciting. Not only do I take the usual responsibility for the content of this book, but I also should emphasize that among those mentioned above some have opposed this approach most vigorously and in their opposition have helped me bring things into focus.

I would venture to say that everyone in ethnographic film—indeed in visual anthropology as a whole—can agree on one thing: that we share our indebtedness to Gregory Bateson and Margaret Mead. Jointly and separately they pioneered in these fields, as in so many other realms of the social sciences, and today, seventy years after they went to Bali, their works are still at the frontier of our discipline. I dedicated the first edition of this book to them. Now I dedicate this second edition to the four ethnographer-filmmakers who most shaped ethnographic film in the second half of the twentieth century.

ETHNOGRAPHIC FILM

ONE

INTRODUCTION

It has been thirty years since I wrote the first edition of this book on ethnographic film. Much has changed in the meantime. It is not just that thousands of new films have been made. More importantly, new video technology has made production much cheaper, has eliminated the need for large
crews on location, and has made sync sound routine. At the same time, in
ethnography itself there has been a growing concern for allowing the voices
of the people to be less filtered through the outside ethnographer. With this
happy conjunction of technological accessibility and theory, we have seen a
proliferation of varieties of ethnographic film. Film is being used to explore
the visual and aural possibilities of ethnography, taking us far beyond the
traditional printed text.

Also, the last quarter century has seen the publication of a large number
of books about ethnographic film, written by filmmakers, anthropologists,
and others. Today many annual, biennial, and occasional conferences on
ethnographic film fill our calendars. And where once the subject was hardly
known and rarely practiced by anyone outside western Europe and North
America, it is now approaching worldwide status.

But even after all the developments of the last decades, we are still working
over some of the same old questions. The first of these is definition.

TOWARD A DEFINITION: THE NATURE OF
THE CATEGORY "ETHNOGRAPHIC FILM"

What do we mean by "ethnographic film"? It is always comfortable to have
a concise definition of title phrases. However, this desire for precision can
often be dangerous. Of all the words that have been spilled over the definition of ethnographic film, most have treated "ethnographic" as an absolute,

present-or-absent characteristic. Let us instead think of "ethnographic" as a continuously variable property of many films. Throughout this book I use the term "ethnographicness" to talk about films. The term is not particularly euphonious, but it does serve notice that "ethnographic" has a very specific meaning.

We can begin with an analogy to "tall buildings." Tallness is obviously an attribute of buildings. Just how tall a building is makes a great deal of difference to an architect, a builder, and an occupant. They all need to have ways to measure and discuss tallness. But it would make no sense at all to attempt to define tall buildings so that some buildings were "tall" and some "not tall." For decades we have spent much energy trying to define ethnographic film in this way. But there is a different approach that is more useful. As long as we phrased the questions in the form "What is an ethnographic film?" or "Is X an ethnographic film?" we were assuming the existence of a bounded category. We had to direct our energies to discovering the boundaries, and we had as our goal the definition of a set of boundary criteria that would allow us to mark off some films as "ethnographic" and, at least implicitly, the rest as "not ethnographic." Certainly the underlying problems are real, but the terms of the inquiry have been sterile. I would suggest a moratorium on such questions.

And now even the tall-buildings analogy becomes inadequate, for "tall" is a single or unidimensional measure. As we talk about films, we must deal with many aspects.

Some have tried to dodge the issue by resorting to broader terms like "documentary film" or "nonfiction film"; some develop specialized terms like "observational cinema" or "transcultural cinema." All of these labels have their uses, but the inherent problem of trying to defend boundaries remains.

So a useful approach is to look for the various attributes, or dimensions, that effect ethnographicness in films. Adopting this strategy, we should ask, "What film features may be more or less ethnographic?" and "In what ways is this film ethnographic?" The idea, then, is not to define an ethnographic box-category but to make explicit those features that contribute to the ethnographicness of films.

There are two overriding considerations:

1. How closely can films approach the highest standards and goals of ethnography?
2. How can films present information that written ethnographies cannot?

To resolve the apparent paradox of these two considerations—being ethnographic and transcending ethnography—we can rephrase them as follows:

How can the (visual capability of) film complement the (lexical capability of) ethnography?

The truism that "a single picture is worth ten thousand words" can be inverted as "a single word can be worth ten thousand pictures." Depending on the situation, either may be true. The challenge of ethnographic film is to develop ways of thinking about film that will make it more ethnographic.

Even though we refuse to define ethnographic film, we must make explicit those attributes that make some films more ethnographic than others. This will make possible a criticism of films from an ethnographic standpoint. More important for the future, it will allow us to explain clearly to ethnographers and to filmmakers how to make films that are more ethnographic and thereby more valuable to anthropology.

In evaluating the degree of ethnographicness in any film, or in designing film projects that are maximally ethnographic, we need to consider a number of attributes, some of which emerge from primarily ethnographic constraints, and some of which emerge from cinematographic constraints. We must stress early and often that when we are talking about "ethnographic film," ethnography must take precedence over cinematography. If ethnographic demands conflict with cinematographic demands, ethnography must prevail.

There are lots of ways to skirt this issue, but it really must be faced head-on. In ethnographic film, film is the tool and ethnography the goal. I have talked with filmmakers who see film as somehow an end in itself, and they reject this idea as demeaning to the art of cinematography. I think that they misunderstand film. It is always a tool for something, and in talking about ethnographic film we are just making that something more explicit than usual. But certainly there is an opposite danger: that anthropologists will see film as "only a tool" and not give it the respect and attention that a fine tool demands. Film-the-tool does some things magnificently well, but for other things it is quite inadequate. We have to understand enough so that we do not try to saw wood with a hammer.

Sometimes this matter is phrased as an inevitable contradiction between art and science, with filmmakers arguing the case for art, and anthropologists the case for science. But this is a distracting approach. The analogy with ethnography-as-literature is pertinent here. We do not demand that an ethnography be written in great literary style. However, when poor writing obscures the ethnographic point, we rightly object. Similarly, although we need not hold ethnographic films to the highest cinematographic standards, a minimal cinematographic competence is required in order that the film communicate at all. In fact, however, it seems safe to say that films that

3

are cinematographically incompetent are also ethnographically incompetent (even when made by an ethnographer). Most of the films we use are far more successful in a technical cinematographic sense than they are in any ethnographic terms. The main problem, and the one to which this book is devoted, is to show filmmakers as well as ethnographers what it means to say that films are ethnographic.

Ethnographic film must be judged in relation to ethnography, which is, after all, a scientific enterprise. In some sense one could argue that all films are "ethnographic": they are about people. Even films that show only clouds or lizards have been made by people and therefore say something about the culture of the individuals who made them and who use them. Many films that have little pretension to ethnographicness are nevertheless of great interest to the ethnographer. I personally feel that *The Last Picture Show,* about the high school class of 1952 in a small Texas town, is a statement that captures the culture of my own high school class of 1952 in Lawrence, Kansas. Likewise, *The Harder They Come* (about Jamaica), *Scenes from a Marriage* (about middle-class Swedish marriage), and *Tokyo Story* (about an extended Japanese family) all present important truths about cultural situations. And I have written elsewhere of how Indonesian feature films are shaped by Indonesian cultural norms (1991a, 1991b). Also, in my cultural anthropology textbook (2004), I have suggested using fiction films that deal with topics of cultural anthropology. As statements (native statements, in fact) about culture, these films are important, and they could serve as raw data or documents in certain kinds of ethnographic research. I am tempted to call them more than just "raw data" and to think of them as "naive ethnography." They have ethnographic import without attempting the science of ethnography. They are good entertainment, but they are also certainly worthy of serious consideration. I have sometimes used such films in my anthropology classes. However, here I want to consider films that are more specifically and intentionally ethnographic.

THE NATURE OF ETHNOGRAPHY

The most important attribute of ethnographic film is the degree to which it is informed by ethnographic understanding. It would be difficult to define "ethnography" in a few words, but we must discuss those features of ethnography that are most relevant to ethnographic filmmaking (and here I shall talk about a general, prototypical sort of ethnography).

First, ethnography is a way of making a detailed description and analysis of human behavior based on a long-term study on the spot. A "come-in-shooting-and-get-out-fast" approach and an intuitive-aesthetic appreciation of behavior and people are other sorts of approaches, and although they may well result in beautiful films, these must inevitably be ethnographically shallow. *The Nuer* is a good example of the limitations of the last approach. It was shot in the late 1960s among a group of Nilotic cattle herders who were living in Ethiopia. Although the filmmakers did spend several months on location and did capture the pace of life in a cattle camp, they missed significant aspects of Nuer ethnography. There is a sequence of the boys' initiation that is dramatic and moving, but from any ethnographic standpoint it is incomplete. On the most obvious level, the two boys are shown leaving boyhood, but their entrance to manhood is omitted except for a slight reference in the narration. The specific important steps in Nuer initiation ceremonies and the structural relation of these ceremonies to rites of passage in general, both of which are well known in ethnographic literature, are hardly touched on in the film. The initiation sequence could have been shaped by these understandings without sacrificing any of the aesthetic qualities of the film. The result would have been stronger ethnographically.

Another essential feature of ethnography is that it relates specific observed behavior to cultural norms. Many documentary films devote much time to the portrayal of an individual person or event but fall short of the cultural step, putting those data into a cultural context. General cultural statements are especially challenging since they must almost inevitably be made in words, whereas film is by nature specific and visual. The difficulty of saying no or asking a question through purely visual means in film or photograph has often been remarked. A photographic generalization is almost as hard to achieve. One of the rare attempts occurs in *The Nuer*, where several quick sequences illustrate various tobacco pipes, ornaments, and scar patterns. The most common solution, used in most films, is to have the narrator read words that put the specific visual images into generalized cultural context. But this forces the film to take on some of the quality of a book, at the expense of the purity of its imagery. There is a real temptation to load too much information into the narration, further weakening the "filmicness" of the film, and at times even contradicting the visual information.

A third basic principle of ethnography is holism. To some degree, things and events must be understood in their social and cultural context. From this principle come the related dicta of "whole bodies," "whole people," "whole interactions," and "whole acts." They emphasize the ethnographic need to present bodies, personalities, and behavior in context. This does not mean that isolated close-ups of body parts (especially faces), fleeting glimpses of impersonalized people, and fragmented representations of behavioral events can never be used, but it recognizes the importance of more holistic shooting.

Like holism itself, "whole people in whole acts" is not a dictum to be followed slavishly. It does not mean that we describe or film everything about everything. A twelve-hour camera's-eye view of life in the village square would not be ethnographically effective. But the holistic principle must be kept in mind as a corrective principle for making films more ethnographic.

Another major feature of ethnography is the goal of truth. On some philosophical level it may be argued that this is a hopelessly naive goal and that reality cannot be truthfully represented. But for our present purposes we can usefully hold that accuracy and truth are essential to ethnography, that some accepted conventional distortions of reality occur in the translation of the living act onto the printed page, and that ethnographers are fairly well aware of the conventions of distortion and are fairly well agreed on what constitutes illegitimate (by name, "dishonest" or "unscientific") distortion.

The conventions of cinematographic honesty are quite different. Cinema has developed primarily as a medium for imaginative statements in which questions of scientific-type accuracy are often irrelevant. Much of what is taught in film schools is how to translate or distort reality for aesthetic effect. These techniques include selective composition of shots, staging acted scenes, editing for continuity effect, and using sound recorded in other contexts. Some of these reality-distorting techniques are inevitable in even the most scrupulously ethnographic films. But in order to understand the ethnographicness of a film, we need to know how much and to what degree reality was distorted. And in making ethnographic films, we can ask that distortions are kept to a minimum and used for ethnographic purposes, not for merely cinematographic reasons. For example, when editing *Dani Houses* and *Dani Sweet Potatoes,* I could have used vaguely appropriate sound recorded two years before I shot my own footage. But I chose not to use this wild sound or any sound other than the narration. As a result, the two films seem tedious and empty to some viewers who expect to be continuously entertained by the sound track. But I had decided, on ethnographic grounds, that the inappropriateness of the wild sound would override the viewing pleasure of audiences accustomed to more technically elaborate films.

Choices of this sort must be made deliberately, not by default. For example, when Donald and Ronald Rundstrom and Clinton Bergum were making *The Path,* they wanted to describe the flow of movement and the use of

6

kinesic energy in the Japanese tea ceremony. To show this with the greatest effectiveness, they shot and edited in a way that lost the casual social gossipy nature of the tea ceremony. The film represents only one side of the reality of the ceremony. But the decisions of what to depict and what to omit were deliberate ethnographic decisions.

These, then, are the ethnographic demands for a general-use ethnographic film, that is, one that is relatively self-explanatory for casual use but demands an accompanying written ethnography for more serious use and deeper understanding. It is difficult to imagine a film that could carry enough ethnographic contextualization and generalization to be fully self-sufficient. At the other extreme, we are now beginning to see some videos that use only synchronous sound, without any generalizing narration. Ethnographically, such films can be extremely effective when used in close connection with a written ethnography or when presented by a well-prepared instructor/informant. But even though they may entirely relegate the generalizing to the written word, the degree to which these films are judged ethnographic must still depend on the degree to which they satisfy the other requirements of ethnographic film discussed above.

To define "ethnographic film" requires either one sentence or an entire book. The sentence is "Ethnographic film is film that reflects ethnographic understanding." This book is an exploration of the nature of ethnographic film. Whatever it is, it is more than the simple sum of ethnography plus film.

It is easy to show the faults in those ethnographic films that are even less than the sum of the two: films made by an ethnographer who happens to take a movie camera into the field, or films made by a filmmaker who happens to wander among an exotic tribe. Often even such films have some documentary value, but they inevitably are monumental missed opportunities. The answer is not simply for a filmmaker to take a course or a degree in anthropology; nor is it enough for an anthropologist to enroll in film school. This is what I mean by emphasizing that ethnographic film is more than the mechanical joining of the two. The effort of thinking cinematically about ethnography or thinking ethnographically through film results in a new and different understanding of each of these disciplines.

Both film and ethnography involve particular ways of viewing the world. Ethnographic film should represent the best of both ethnography and film. This can be done by respecting the constraints of each discipline and taking advantage of the opportunities and insights of each. All this is just saying—in abstract, programmatic phrases—that which the rest of this book makes explicit.

THE DIFFERING NATURES OF
ETHNOGRAPHY AND FILM

There are profound differences between ethnography and film that are corollaries of the obvious differences between word-on-paper versus photo-on-celluloid or image-on-videotape. Having said that the differences begin with word versus picture, I will examine the consequences of these differences, and in particular how all this affects the way in which people go about the two enterprises.

The ethnographic research that culminates in a book and the filmmaking that culminates in a film are quite different enterprises that can be schematized as follows:

The ethnographer	The filmmaker
Begins with theoretical problems and research plans	Begins with an idea and a script
Gathers data by making observations and asking questions	Shoots footage
Analyzes data	Edits footage
Writes and rewrites	
Produces a written report	Produces a film

Cinematography makes irreversible choices at the very beginning. The finished film can contain only those images that were shot at the beginning. Especially in ethnographic filmmaking, where the shooting is done in the field and is completed before the editing begins, the editing stage is one of manipulating a finite amount of set material. Scenes can be shortened, thrown out, or their sequence juggled, and titles and narration can be added. But, practically speaking, new footage cannot be created at the editing table.

Imagine for a moment a comparable situation in ethnography. The ethnographer spends a few months in the field, writing down observations in notebooks. Then she returns home, makes a photocopy of the notebook, and with scissors and paste proceeds to fashion an ethnography out of the sentences and paragraphs she wrote down in the field. She can take sentences from different pages of the notebook and juxtapose them into new paragraphs. But she cannot write any new words or sentences.

In reality the ethnographer writes and rewrites, analyzes and reanalyzes; in short, she composes and recomposes words into sentences, and sentences into paragraphs. The final ethnography hardly contains a single phrase as originally set down in the first field record. On the other hand, except for a few printed titles, the final ethnographic film contains only images that were originally photographed. The basic difference in the way in which understanding enters the process is dramatically illustrated by the fact that when the footage has been shot, someone other than the photographer can (and usually does) edit it into the finished film, but it would be almost impossible to write an ethnography from someone else's field notes.

This difference between editing (the film) and rewriting (the book) has several implications. First, whereas the thorough understanding of what is going on often emerges only at the end of the ethnographic process, it must precede the filmmaking. Of course, the ethnographer must begin gathering data with some research plan in mind. But actually, many of the most important data are gathered on the fringe, so to speak, by means other than the pre-established research procedures. The peripheral vision of the anthropologist is often an extremely important research tool. We rarely talk about it or systematize it, but we do use it. Also, as anthropologists come to understand the behavior of a people better, they can retrieve data from their own memories or from the memories of their informants. Such convenient hindsight is of no help to the cinematographer. Time past cannot be refilmed. A ceremony is filmed on the basis of whatever understanding (and luck) the filmmakers had at the moment of filming. (And I would insist that "lucky shots" are usually the rewards of understanding.) Later, when the filmmakers know more, they can film a different ceremony, and they can cut and shuffle the old footage. They can edit, but they cannot rewrite.

Ethnographic understanding emerges from the analysis, and an ethnography is only as good as the analysis. But an ethnographic film can only be as good as the understanding that precedes the filmmaking. Or, put another way, the degree to which a film is ethnographic depends on the degree to which prior ethnographic understanding has informed the filmmaking. This is the most basic message of this entire book, and I shall repeat it often in different ways.

Filmmaking is not quite so rigidly locked into first impressions as the preceding lines might suggest, but the qualifications only strengthen the argument. Often in ethnographic filmmaking, we find a wordy narration used as a bridge, or a bandage, to patch over a gap in the footage where some sequence has not been fully filmed. Often this gap is the result of ignorance, where the cameraman has not understood well enough what was going on to be able to anticipate and to shoot satisfactory footage. The inability to anticipate meant that the camera batteries went dead, or the camera was unloaded at the crucial moment (I shot an important scene for *Dead Birds* with an unloaded camera), or the cameraman was not even present. But it is significant, in the context of this argument, that the filmic gap is frequently closed by words. When this is done, then the filmicness of the film is diminished, and the product edges toward a spoken book. We have already insisted that ethnographic films be maximally ethnographic; but ethnographic films should also be maximally visual.

"TRUTH" IN FILM AND ETHNOGRAPHY

A basic problem, already mentioned in this chapter, that runs through all considerations of ethnographic film concerns the nature of truth. Filmmakers and ethnographers, when they think of it at all, take quite different positions on truth. Certainly everyone subscribes to truth. No one really advocates untruth. (Those who deny the very possibility of truth remove themselves from this discussion.) But filmmakers can comfortably take the artists' position that they manipulate reality through a series of falsehoods in order to create a higher truth. This appeal to higher truth has been made in more or less epigrammatic form, by all sorts of artists. Anthropologists, as scientists, assume that they must challenge the legitimacy of these facilitating lies. In science, the end cannot justify the means: results are only as sound as the methodology that produces them. Nice words. But if we look a bit more closely, we see that anthropologists have their own methodological conventions for reaching truth. And we should be rather explicit about them.

If one were to ask anthropologists to name the five best ethnographies, or the five that they liked best, one would have no trouble getting lists from most anthropologists. Actually, "five best" might be too much of an American-specific concept, and one might have to rephrase the question for anthropologists of other cultures—for example, "five really first-rate ethnographies." But lists would still be forthcoming. If one next asked the same anthropologists if truth was important to ethnography, the response would be a nearly unanimous yes. But then if one asked for a list of the five truest, or most accurate ethnographies, there would be trouble. People would hesitate and ask for clarification, and if they produced a list at all, it would not overlap much with their list of the "five best."

Assuming that I am correct about the thinking of my anthropological colleagues, what is going on here? One important difference between the five best and the five truest ethnographies would probably be that the "truest" were safe catalogs of trait lists, while the best were works that did not attempt any sort of exhaustive coverage. Rather, they would take a selection of data and interpret these data in a particularly enlightening and convincing manner. The truth perhaps, but certainly not the whole truth.

In short, we do not really expect any ethnography (or film) to say everything about a subject. This means that there must be selection and there must be omission. Therefore, the value of an ethnography or a film cannot be judged on the basis of whether or not it has omitted things. Rather, it must be judged on the appropriateness of what has been included and how the content has been handled.

All this must seem obvious, but in actual practice it is easy to forget. For example, many anthropologists criticized Robert Gardner's film *Dead Birds* on the grounds that it showed only the men's side of Dani life. When it was pointed out that many women's activities were in fact shown, the criticism was modified to "Well, he didn't show enough of the women." Gardner's later film *Rivers of Sand* concerns the role of women among the Hamar of Ethiopia and is dominated by the statements of one Hamar woman. Now the criticism is reversed: Gardner doesn't present the men's side. It would be small wonder if Gardner felt frustrated by these criticisms. Underlying them is the feeling that somehow a film *should* cover everything. But that is a feeling held by anthropologists who would not make such a demand of ethnographies.

There is another convention that anthropologists accept in written ethnographies but often challenge in films. That convention is the common device of reconstructing an account of an event from diverse data in order to make a single, reasonable, typical, "true" account. When audiences learn that the giraffe hunt in *The Hunters* was constructed in the editing room out of scenes from several different hunts, or that the battle sequence in *Dead Birds* combined footage shot at different battles, they often feel betrayed and lose confidence in the total description of a Bushman hunt or a Dani battle.

But, in fact, a comparable construction is done in ethnography—for example, in Bronislaw Malinowski's *Argonauts of the Western Pacific* (1922). This is one of the earliest and still one of the most respected ethnographies. It would certainly appear in nearly every anthropologist's "five best ethnographies" list, discussed earlier.

The middle section of that book describes a long trading expedition undertaken by the Trobriand Islanders from their homes in Sinaketa, in the north, to Dobu, an island to the south. Now, Malinowski had not actually participated in any such expedition. His account is reconstructed from brief observations of somewhat similar events and from accounts that he gathered from his Trobriand informants. His defense of this technique is worth quoting at some length, because in so many ways Malinowski laid the foundation for ethnographic fieldwork and is still a powerful role model for ethnographers:

> In the twelve preceding chapters, we have followed an expedition from Sinaketa to Dobu. . . . As I have seen, indeed followed, a big *uvalaku* expedition from the South to the Trobriands, I shall be able to give some of the scenes from direct impression, and not from reconstruction. Such a reconstruction for one who has seen much of the natives' tribal life and has a good grip over intelligent informants is neither very difficult nor need it be fanciful at all. Indeed, towards the end of my second visit, I had several times opportunities to check such a reconstruction by witnessing the actual occurrence, for after my first year's stay in the Trobriands I had written out already some of my material. As a rule, even in minute details, my reconstructions hardly differed from reality, as the tests have shown. None the less, it is possible for an ethnographer to enter into concrete details with more conviction when he describes things actually seen. (Malinowski 1922, 376)

This sort of reconstruction of an event in written description is an accepted convention in ethnography. It is not exclusively used, of course. Malinowski himself brought in rich specific case studies, or anecdotes, as well as these generalized reconstructions. The point is that the general reconstruction, when used properly, is a legitimate ethnographic descriptive device. But there are differences between print and film uses of this convention. A good example is the housebuilding of the Dani. I have described Dani construction in print (1970, 261–263) and in film (*Dani Houses,* 1974). During the years that I lived in West New Guinea with the Dani, I observed (and often participated in) housebuilding, but I never saw all the steps in building any one house. I formed a complete picture of Dani construction from countless isolated observations of Dani at work. I am now somewhat embarrassed to realize that I never actually wrote these qualifications in my ethnography. And my account is phrased in very general terms. It begins: "The main part of the construction is done by the men and boys who will live in the men's house. Chopping of lumber and actual construction is done only by men; women carry wood and thatch grass to the site . . ." (1970, 261).

I did not tell the reader where I got my information. But presumably most readers would understand this as a general account. And, in contrast, when I later discussed "magic associated with housebuilding," I was very careful not to claim these data as general, specifying the names of the compound sites: "At Anisimo a knot of grass . . . At Biem, dried banana leaf was wrapped around the base . . . At Musanima . . ." (1970, 263). In the film *Dani Houses,* I used footage of that instance of banana leaf magic mentioned in this quotation. However, although in the book it is clear that I observed that banana leaf magic only once, I did not put this information into the narration of the film. And, in fact, most viewers would probably assume that such banana leaf magic was a standard part of Dani housebuilding. On the surface this is a minor ethnographic detail, but such situations are multiplied many times in the course of any ethnographic film, and the problem of truth becomes a major consideration.

Also, while shooting the film *Dani Houses,* I had missed several steps in the sequences. But during the editing, I made the decision not to edit diverse shots together for continuity but rather to keep them separate, in the order in which they had occurred. For example, the first sequence in the film follows the construction of two pigsties. I had footage of women carrying the thatch grass to the construction site, but I did not get footage of the grass being plucked. For a later sequence, there is footage of both the plucking and the carrying to the site of a round house. I decided to use the plucking footage in the second sequence, where it belonged. But that means that we first see thatch grass appear without knowing how it was gathered. It would have made for a smoother, more logical film to have used the plucking footage in the first sequence. But since that footage was of different people in a different place, I held out for accuracy.

There was yet another dilemma in *Dani Houses.* I had filmed half the construction of a men's round house and then, through some circumstances not relevant to the housebuilding itself, I missed the completion of that house. Later I filmed the second half of the construction of a women's round house. It would have been possible, by choosing proper shooting angles, and through editing, to present the two houses as one. Instead I deliberately emphasized that they were separate and mentioned the differences between men's and women's houses.

These sorts of specific, demystifying approaches are becoming more common in ethnography as well as in ethnographic film. We have seen that Malinowski, writing in the 1920s and 1930s, used both the specific illustration and the generalized description. My own 1970 monograph is somewhat more generalizing than Malinowski's works, while my films (finished several years after the monograph) represent more uncompromising specifics. Of course, words lend themselves to generalizing statements more easily than does film, whereas the specificity of the film image makes filmic generalizations less satisfactory and more manipulative.

In written accounts we usually have some idea of the extent to which a description is specific, reconstructed, or generalized. The choice of verb form and the use of parenthetical expressions, footnotes, and explanatory paragraphs offer opportunities to qualify or support written data. We usually do not get comparable information in films. It is more difficult to slip parenthetical information into a film. When a description must be seen from beginning to end at a predetermined speed, without pause or backtracking, there is no place for a footnote. Of course, it would still be possible to include qualifying information in a film, but it would be more intrusive and the conventions of filmmaking are against it.

TWO

A HISTORY OF
ETHNOGRAPHIC FILM

Any history of ethnographic film is bound to be someone's selective story. Many somewhat different stories have been told, but this is my version. It begins with a prehistory of gifted adventurers like Martin and Osa Johnson, Merian C. Cooper, Ernest B. Schoedsack, and, towering above them all, Robert Flaherty. They knew little or nothing about ethnography but used film to bring the images of distant peoples to audiences in North America and Europe. This history proper begins with the Balinese studies of Gregory Bateson and Margaret Mead. It dwells on the seminal works of four men who were active for most of the second half of the twentieth century: Jean Rouch, John Marshall, Robert Gardner, and Timothy Asch. By focusing on these four, we can see the shape of ethnographic film.

So this chapter is a very selective historical sketch of the development of ethnographic film, intended to show what was learned, as well as what has been allowed to slip from our awareness since the 1920s. It is based on those films that I happened to have been able to see and study in the United States. And it is a historical prologue to the next chapter.

The history of ethnographic film is one part of the history of cinematography itself and, more particularly, of documentary, or nonfiction film. Both film and ethnography were born in the nineteenth century and reached their maturity in the 1920s. But curiously enough, it was not until the 1960s that film and ethnography systematically began to join in effective collaboration. The few earlier exceptions had little impact on either film or ethnography. By the twenty-first century this later development, which was once centered in the United States, France, Australia, and, to a much lesser degree, Great Britain, has spread around the world.

However, we shall see that, during the first forty years of ethnographic film, the major contributions were made by people who were outside (or uncomfortably on the fringe of) the film industry and by others who were more or less peripheral to anthropology.

BACKGROUND FACTORS

Before diving into this history of ethnographic film, we should at least mention several factors that lie behind its development, namely, cinema technology, the economics of filmmaking, and the development of ethnography.

Cinema Technology and the Economics of Filmmaking

By the beginning of the twentieth century, the basic cinema technology that was a prerequisite to ethnographic film was available. By the mid-1960s, synchronous sound-film equipment was portable enough and reliable enough to be used in even the most remote regions. And by 1970 we had fully portable videotape equipment. The first development was, of course, essential to any ethnographic filming; the second development, lightweight synchronous sound equipment, allowed simultaneous recording of the visual and aural aspects of an event. This created an important new dimension of reality and allowed the filmmaker to avoid the pitfalls of narration and postsynchronized background sounds. But the synchronous sound equipment remained expensive and required a team: minimally, one person to operate the camera and another to run the tape recorder.

The third development, videotape, has the great advantage of instant playback with synchronous sound. And videotape's capacity for making long takes without stopping to rewind or reload allows camera operators to capture important moments of spontaneous behavior, something so much more a matter of luck with a movie camera. By the twenty-first century, video cameras and editing equipment had increased in quality and dropped in cost so that even graduate students on grants could afford to use them.

The Development of Ethnography

The 1920s saw the firm establishment of fieldwork-based ethnography and the responsible popularization of ethnographic insights. Many important ethnographic monographs had been published earlier, but 1922 was a landmark year: both A. R. Radcliffe-Brown's *Andaman Islanders* and Bronislaw Malinowski's *Argonauts of the Western Pacific* were published. These men were to dominate British anthropology for the next two decades. Malinowski wrote several more monographs on the Trobriand Islanders. His books had provocative titles (e.g., *The Sexual Life of Savages*) and an easy style, and they were read far beyond the borders of academic anthropology. In the United

States, the gap between academic and popular was being bridged even more successfully by Margaret Mead and later Ruth Benedict.

Mead had carried out research in Samoa in 1925–1926. Her monograph *Social Organization of Manua* (1930b) was written for her colleagues, but in *Coming of Age in Samoa* (1928) she had attempted to make her Samoan data relevant to current concerns in the United States. In her later work in New Guinea, Mead followed the same pattern: technical monographs for the profession, and relevant ethnographies for the public, addressed to problems like child rearing, education, and sex roles. Then, in 1934, came Ruth Benedict's *Patterns of Culture,* which further synthesized and popularized anthropology.

Certainly, Mead had established the validity of popular professional ethnography, which could encompass both solid scientific research and responsible popularization. But anthropologists made no attempt in that decade to use film for comparable purposes.

For reasons of geographical accident at least, Robert Flaherty's first two films should have been of particular personal interest to American anthropologists. *Nanook of the North* was made on the eastern shore of the Hudson Bay, some seven hundred miles south of Baffin Island, where Franz Boas, the dominant figure in American anthropology, had spent a year in 1883–1884. Although by 1922, when *Nanook* was finished, Boas had become primarily concerned with Northwest Coast Indians, he must have had continuing interest in Eskimos. And Flaherty made his second film, *Moana,* on Savaii, in Western Samoa—less than three hundred miles from Manua, in Eastern Samoa, where Margaret Mead, who had been one of Boas's students, did her fieldwork. *Moana* was first shown in New York in 1926, while Mead was in Samoa, but she had heard of the film even while she was in the field (see Mead 1972, 154). It is hard to imagine that Flaherty's films were not seen by anthropologists (see Ruby 2000, 83ff). But if Boas, Mead, and the other American anthropologists even saw Flaherty's films, there is no indication that they appreciated their ethnographic implications. (However, as we shall see, Mead did play a major role in the development of ethnographic film. But if she or anyone else was inspired by Flaherty's films, they did not mention it in print.)

In short, despite the availability of cinema technology since the turn of the century, despite the popular models since the 1920s, and perhaps because of financial problems before the 1960s, anthropology did not contribute to ethnographic film in any systematic and sustained way during the early decades.

The history of the four decades from the 1920s to the 1960s is marked by only a few real achievements in ethnographic film. A good deal of footage was shot. Some of this is preserved in the German archives at Göttingen, and more is held in Washington, D.C., at the National Anthropological Film Center at the Smithsonian Institution and at the Library of Congress.

PREHISTORY: THE EXPLORERS

It is always satisfying to have some definite date with which to begin a history. For ethnographic film, Jean Rouch (1970, 13) suggests that it should be 4 April 1901. On that day Baldwin Spencer, who was to become famous for his studies of the Australian Aborigines, shot footage of an Aborigine kangaroo dance and a rain ceremony. The few other ethnographic films, or films on tribal peoples, that were made before 1922 may be mentioned in passing (see O'Reilly 1970). The Hamburg South Sea Expedition of 1908–1910 made a twenty-minute film on various topics, especially dances, in Micronesia and Melanesia. In 1912, Gaston Méliês, brother of the important cinema pioneer Georges, made some short films of the sort that Patrick O'Reilly calls "documentaires romancés" in Tahiti and New Zealand (1970). In 1914, Edward Curtis, famous for his sensitive romantic photographic portraits of American Indians, made a scripted epic of the Kwakiutl Indians, which has recently been restored and re-released under the title *In the Land of the War Canoes.*

Martin and Osa Johnson

During the fifteen years from 1917 until Martin's death in a plane crash, Martin and Osa Johnson became two of the most famous Americans, and Osa's 1940 autobiography, *I Married Adventure,* was a Book-of-the-Month Club selection. The Johnsons' careers have been chronicled extensively in the biographies by Imperato and Imperato (1992) and others (Stott 1978; Arruda 2001), and their films have received some serious attention from anthropologists (Lindstrom 2005; Prins 1992).

Martin had led a charmed life. In 1906, at the age of twenty-three, he talked his way onto a round-the-world expedition organized by the author Jack London, who was building a boat called *Snark.* The expedition explored Polynesian islands and reached the Solomon Islands, but it ended abruptly in November 1908 when London became debilitated by tropical ailments.

Martin returned to the United States and developed a career as theatrical entrepreneur, lecturer, and writer based in his hometown of Independence, Kansas. He used materials on the Pacific from the *Snark* trip. In 1910 he eloped with Osa, a sixteen-year-old from the nearby town of Chanute. For the next seven years they followed the vaudeville circuit as one of many travel shows incorporating film footage of exotic places. Finally, in 1917, they put together financing for their own expedition to Melanesia to pick up where Martin had left off a decade earlier. For the next four years they were involved with filming tribal peoples in Melanesia and Borneo. They then turned to East and Central Africa to make animal films, only returning to Borneo in 1935 to film and capture orangutans. Their numerous books and films were widely distributed at the time, and there remains a remarkable monument to their work, the Martin and Osa Johnson Safari Museum in Chanute.

They had been preceded by the displays of "native villages" featuring real people at world fairs and exhibitions in the nineteenth century (see Rony 1996). The Midway, just outside the gates of the 1893 World's Columbian Exhibition in Chicago boasted not only Buffalo Bill's Wild West Show with more than two hundred Indians and cavalry from several nations but also numerous "natives" from around the world (Larson 2003). Millions of people came to these fairs to gawk, but the movies of the Johnsons and others would reach millions more.

The Johnsons and other such camera-wielding adventurers were bringing moving images of very foreign peoples to wide publics in North American and Europe during the years just before 1922. In no sense would we now call these products ethnographic films, but certainly they created a wide awareness of the exotic. For better or worse, they set the stage for Robert Flaherty's 1922 film, *Nanook of the North.*

One particular accomplishment of the Johnsons' stands out: showing footage back to the subjects. It happened this way. The Johnsons had visited the people called the Big Nambas on the island of Malekula in search of cannibals. A film of a real cannibal feast was the ultimate dream of the period. Although the Johnsons seem never to have quite succeeded in filming cannibalism, they did describe in harrowing detail their narrow escape from a village of enraged natives (Johnson 1940, 119–124). Even encumbered by camera, tripod, and supplies, the Johnsons managed to outrace the natives down the jungle hillside and were rescued by their waiting whaleboat. The Imperatos (1992, 73) suggest that the Johnsons may have exaggerated their peril. At any rate, the couple had come away with footage that was made into a film called *Among the Cannibal Isles of the South Seas.* First as a lecture film accompanied by the Johnsons, then as a feature release with intertitles, it was a great success under the title of *Cannibals of the South Seas.*

In 1919 the Johnsons launched another expedition, returned to Malekula, and shot footage of the Big Nambas watching themselves as the Johnsons

19

screened the film for them. Footage of this event was included in their next Melanesian feature film, *Head Hunters of the South Seas,* which was released in 1922.

As it happened, the Johnsons were making their early films at the same time that Robert Flaherty was shooting the footage for *Nanook,* and both released films in 1922. The Johnsons were enterprising adventurers whose films were mainly about themselves, the wonders they had seen, and the dangers they had passed. Even the remarkable idea of filming the Big Nambas watching a film about themselves (Johnson 1940, 134–137) was nothing more than a gimmick to further cast them as credulous savages.

Martin and Osa Johnson were the exemplary adventurer-explorers of their time, although there were many others like them (see Griffiths 2002 and Kaplan 1984). Through their numerous films, books, and lectures, they and the others brought a new awareness of tribal peoples and exotic animals to the Western public. From today's perspective they were hopelessly ethnocentric, reinforcing Western concepts of tribal peoples as savages. But the Johnsons, toward the end of their careers, abandoned the search for headhunters and cannibals and turned to the great East African herds, and the couple came to have respect for tribal people whose local knowledge of the animals was so much greater than that of any "white hunter."

But meanwhile, in a career that was almost exactly contemporaneous with that of Martin and Osa Johnson, a mining engineer from Canada named Robert Flaherty was developing a very different way to film exotic people.

Robert Flaherty

If ethnographic film was conceived in 1901 when Baldwin Spencer shot his first footage of Australian Aborigines, it was born on 11 June 1922, when Robert Flaherty's Inuit (Eskimo) film, *Nanook of the North,* opened in a New York theater. The film became an immediate success and was seen by audiences around the world. But *Nanook's* success was singular. It did not really open the doors for ethnographic film or even for Robert Flaherty, who had great problems financing new film projects. *Nanook* has always been a great landmark. When I took introductory anthropology courses in the mid-1950s, before *The Hunters* was released, *Nanook* and two of Flaherty's other films, *Moana* and *Man of Aran,* were practically the only films used in anthropology courses. However, by the twenty-first century, with hundreds of ethnographic films available, Flaherty's films are rarely seen.

Many details of Flaherty's life are cloaked in the myths that he spun about them during his lifetime and that his admirers repeated after his death. One approaches him through his biographies (Griffith 1953; Calder-Marshall 1963;

Rotha and Wright 1980; Danzker 1980; Rotha 1983; Barsam 1988; Ruby 2000), with a mixture of confusion and amusement. But myths aside, his accomplishments were real.

Flaherty was a mining engineer and an explorer. Like the physicist Boas in Baffinland, and the marine biologist Alfred Haddon in the Torres Strait, Flaherty went to the field in the interests of a traditional science and found that his attention turned from the things of sea and land to the people who lived there. He lived in Inuit country and traveled with Inuit for long periods between 1910 and 1921. In 1914 he shot his first Inuit footage, but it was destroyed in a fire. The Flaherty legend tells of a careless cigarette that ignited the highly flammable nitrate-based film stock. Arthur Calder-Marshall (1963, 74) is probably right in his assessment of the incident: it saved Flaherty from trying to sell an amateurish film, and it sent him back to film *Nanook*. Returning to Hudson Bay, Flaherty shot the footage for *Nanook* in 1921–1922, and it was finished in the summer of 1922. The next year he went to Samoa to try to repeat the success of *Nanook*. His Samoan film, *Moana: A Romance of the Golden Age,* was released in 1926, but it never had the phenomenal commercial success of *Nanook*. During the next years he made two more trips to Polynesia to assist other directors in fictional romances but each time withdrew from the project before the film was finished. Flaherty shot his third major film on the Aran Islands, off the west coast of Ireland, between 1931 and 1933, and *Man of Aran* was released in 1934. In 1935 he again ventured into purely commercial filmmaking, this time *Elephant Boy,* in India. Flaherty stayed with this film to the end, but his contributions were finally overwhelmed by the producer, and the result was not a "Flaherty film." In 1939–1941 he made *The Land* under U.S. government contract, about the American agricultural depression. But *The Land* generated great political opposition and has never been widely distributed. His last film, *Louisiana Story,* shot in 1946–1948, was released in 1948, and at the time of his death in 1951 he was planning a film on Hawaii.

It is clear that Flaherty's accomplishments were achieved at tremendous personal cost. He tried to function in the world of commercial film, but his films were too ethnographic for that, and his ethnography was too naive and self-invented to give him access to academia. But even though Flaherty had little effect on later ethnographic films, several aspects of his approach should be recognized.

INTENSIVE IMMERSION

Although Flaherty was no ethnographer and did not pretend to approach cultures with an ethnographic research plan, he did spend an extended time in the field for each film, observing and absorbing the native culture. He was no fly-by-night explorer. He lived in Inuit country for much of eleven years (about twelve months while shooting *Nanook*), in Samoa for one and a half years, Ireland for one and a half years, and more than one year in the Louisiana bayous. His commitment to something like the ethnographic technique of personal immersion in a culture was remarkable. Frances Flaherty's description of how the couple went about making *Moana* (Griffith 1953, 52–71) is similar to a description of an ethnographic field trip. The Flahertys were not just living in Samoa; they were constantly searching, looking, and trying to understand Samoan life. Although length of stay does not guarantee depth of knowledge, it is a fairly essential precondition. Fleeting visits and shallow knowledge are all too evident in many later ethnographic films.

THE DRAMA OF THE SPECIFIC INDIVIDUAL: WHOLE PEOPLE

Flaherty understood the implications of film as specific, contrasted with the printed word as general. He used his films to make generalizations by following the specific acts of a specific individual: he made films that focused on Nanook, the Inuit man; on Moana, the Samoan youth; and on the Man of Aran. He tried to do more than just give us faceless unidentified Inuit or Samoans or Irishmen. He pushed film to its filmic specific limit, letting the audience enjoy and identify with a real, albeit exotic, individual. This may be Flaherty's most important contribution to ethnographic film, and its influence is clear in *The Hunters* and *Dead Birds*. It is safe to say that no ethnographic film has suffered from focusing too much on an individual, and many are flawed by not doing so.

Flaherty tried to tell a story: not, as in novels or scripted film, a story of human interaction or passion or the search for love or wealth or power, but a story of the individual facing crisis. In *Nanook* it was man's struggle with nature; in Samoa, where nature was too beneficent, it was Moana against his culture, bearing the pain of the tattooing process that would make him a man; and in Ireland it was again man against nature, the Man of Aran against the sea. (Women were always incidental in Flaherty's films.)

RECONSTRUCTION AND THE ETHNOGRAPHIC PRESENT

Flaherty ventured into one of the more treacherous realms of ethnography. He created artifice to assert a truth. He convinced the Samoan youth to undergo a tattooing ceremony that had nearly died out; he persuaded the Aran Islanders to re-create their hunt for the basking sharks, a skill they had not practiced for a generation or more. To film Eskimo life inside an igloo, Flaherty had the Eskimo build an igloo set; it was a half-dome, twice life-size. In fact, very little of his final footage was of spontaneous behavior. The validity of these filmic distortions and their relationship to the accepted distortion of written ethnography are at the crux of the major criticism of Flaherty's ethnographic films. His films are obviously attractive and interesting, but are they true? Flaherty met this issue head-on. Calder-Marshall quotes him as saying, "Sometimes you have to lie. One often has to distort a thing to catch its true spirit" (1963, 97). We will consider this question and its implications in the next chapter.

NATIVE FEEDBACK

The Flaherty legend relates how Flaherty developed his footage each evening and screened it for his subjects, getting their reactions and advice and thus making them real collaborators in the filmmaking process. This is a fascinating idea. It has the potentially great advantage of making film more truly reflective of the natives' insight into their own culture. Flaherty may have first showed his footage to his Inuit friends as entertainment. But Jay Ruby has documented how Flaherty developed a real collaboration with the Inuit (e.g., 2000, 87–91). As they came to understand his goals, they offered suggestions for making his film more truly reflective of their own insights into their culture. It is not at all clear if Flaherty even tried this approach in his later film projects in Samoa or Ireland. Many ethnographic filmmakers since Flaherty have thought about this sort of collaboration, no one more effectively than Jean Rouch and Timothy Asch, as we shall discuss later.

Another sort of native feedback did come out of Flaherty's stay in Ireland. Pat Mullen, the Aran Islander who was Flaherty's "contact man" during the filming and appeared in the film, wrote a book about his experiences with Flaherty. It was called, like the film, *Man of Aran* (1935). This book was a remarkable document in ethnographic film. It is matched only by Pat Loud's book (1974) describing her experiences as the mother and wife of *An American Family,* a twelve-part television documentary produced by Craig Gilbert for National Educational Television.

VISUAL SUSPENSE

In the 1920s, of course, Flaherty was limited to silent film. He could, and did, occasionally stop the visual film to insert an intertitle, but he was spared by the technology of his time from the temptation to overnarrate. Thus, he was forced to think visually. Also, to the extent that he screened rushes while in the field, he knew what he had on film and could do additional shooting immediately. He did not have to bridge over missing shots with narration.

As a trained engineer, Flaherty was fascinated by the local knowledge of the Inuit. One of Flaherty's most successful visual techniques was to follow an exotic act visually, showing it step by step as it developed, not explaining it in words. In one sequence of *Nanook* we see Nanook tugging on a line that leads into a hole in the ice. We are engaged in that act and think about it. Eventually, the suspense is broken: our questions are answered when Nanook pulls out a seal. Flaherty creates the same visual involvement when Nanook makes the igloo—especially at the end of the sequence, when Nanook cuts a slab of ice for a window, sets it in place, and fixes a snow slab reflector along one side. For a time we are puzzled and therefore involved. But when Nanook steps back, finished, we understand.

Flaherty also used this technique in *Moana* in the sequences of snaring a wild pig and smoking a robber crab out of the rocks. In both sequences, we are told that there is something to be caught, we see the technology involved, and finally we see the catch. In fact, the robber crab sequence has a mystery within a mystery. As the boy sets about to catch the something, he kindles a fire by rubbing a small stick along a groove cut into a larger branch. For viewers who are not familiar with this device, called a fire plow in the ethnographic literature, the mystery is resolved only when the boy blows the embers into flame.

In this way, as Calder-Marshall points out (1963, 95), Flaherty makes demands on his audience: he demands that they join him in observing the Eskimo. It is very revealing to compare the 1922 version of *Nanook* with a later one, released in 1947, four years before Flaherty's death. Now the film has been speeded up by 50 percent, from 16 frames per second to 24 frames per second to accommodate sound. Where the titles with their few sparse words once were, the scenes now fade out to black and fade in to the next sequence; worse, we are subjected to a steady narration, backed by orchestral music and sounds of wind howling and dogs barking. The narration adds little information, but the steady barrage of words anticipates needlessly and comments gratuitously. In the original version, we participated in Nanook's window and admired its ingenuity; now the narrator tells us how ingenious it is and what a skilled person Nanook is. There is the great irony: one must assume that Flaherty himself collaborated in, or at least assented to, the speeded-up sound version.

GRASS

In retrospect, Robert Flaherty dominates the ethnographic film of the 1920s on the grounds not only of the quality of his films but also of the insight of his approach. But one cannot discuss the 1920s without considering the film *Grass,* shot by Merian C. Cooper and Ernest B. Schoedsack in 1924 and released in 1925. Cooper and Schoedsack had earlier shot footage in Ethiopia for a film about Haile Selassie, but, in a curious echo of Flaherty's experience with his first Inuit film, their undeveloped negative was destroyed by a ship fire (Behlmer 1966, 19). Like Flaherty, they were not diverted from filmmaking, and in 1924 they went to the Near East to make a film about exploration. They wandered around, shooting superficial travelogue footage until they reached Persia, where they joined the Bakhtiari herdsmen on their annual trek from winter to summer pastures. This is a nomadic-like pattern that is called transhumance. Cooper and Schoedsack's approach had little of the sophistication of Flaherty's. Cooper and Schoedsack apparently spent only a couple of months with the Bakhtiari and only peripherally focused on individuals—the khan and his son. (Behlmer, who interviewed Cooper [1966], states that they had planned to make a second migration with the Bakhtiari, this time to film a single family, but that they ran short of funds and finished the film with only the more general footage of the first trip.)

Most of *Grass* follows the remarkable movement of hundreds of people and thousands of animals across a wide icy river and over a steep snowy mountain range. This is in no sense a reconstruction, dependent on the filmmakers' understanding. They were obviously permitted to participate in the Bakhtiari's march and to film what they could. Neither Flaherty nor any later filmmaker ever found a man-against-nature drama that could match this in terms of sheer visual spectacle. What begins as a routine travel film becomes almost by accident an unsurpassed spontaneous drama. The film now seems dated because the intertitles are too often merely cute. And we learn little of the cultural background of the Bakhtiari. Even the book Cooper wrote (1925) is more about the adventure than the Bakhtiari. Indeed, anticipating that the single trek will seem unbelievable, the film opens with a photograph of a statement notarized by the American consul in Shiraz, stating that they did make the trek. We are not even told that this is a yearly migration. It is almost as if our credulity has been strained by seeing it even once. But despite its many faults as ethnography, *Grass* remains a classic bit of ethnographic data.

SCRIPTED FICTIONAL FILMS

In the late 1920s and early 1930s a number of films were shot in exotic locations, using local people to act out written fictional scripts with strong plotlines. This was a logical step beyond Flaherty's directed reconstructions in

25

Canada, Samoa, and Ireland. In another sense, it was a logical step from the commercial films, which then, as now, used natives (of Europe or the United States) to act out fictional themes from their own cultures. The "Hollywood film" was and is the epitome of this approach.

These early films were commercial ventures, taking advantage of the public interest that had been stimulated by filmmakers like Flaherty and ethnographers like Mead. But because the actors could be controlled by directors and script, these films could be made without the risks and uncertainties of documentary film. Flaherty himself became involved in this type of filmmaking. In 1927 he went to Tahiti with W. S. Van Dyke to film *White Shadows in the South Seas* (1928). But the two men apparently could not work together, and Flaherty withdrew. The next year he returned to French Polynesia with the famous German director F. W. Murnau to make *Tabu* (1931), and again there were problems and Flaherty left. The stories of personal friction during these two ventures make good movie gossip. But it is more interesting to look at the differences between these two scripted films, which Flaherty rejected, and the films that Flaherty did on his own. *Nanook, Moana,* and *Man of Aran* all purport to show untouched, untroubled cultures. In *Nanook* the brief scenes at the fur trading post are used for benign humor and to satisfy the fur company that paid for the film. (We see Nanook listening in wonderment to a phonograph, and he tests a record with his teeth in a scene that always draws a laugh.) There is no consideration of how the intrusion of fur traders and all their cultural baggage may have affected the Eskimos.

But while Flaherty pictures the brave-and-noble-savage in the Arctic, Samoa, and Ireland, the Polynesian films of Van Dyke and Murnau show the noble-savage-corrupted-by-civilization. In fact, in *Tabu* everyone gets into the act: a weak French colonial officer, a European trader, a dishonest Chinese saloonkeeper, and a relentless Polynesian chief all conspire to thwart the love of the young Polynesian couple. In both sorts of films the use of idealized cultural stereotypes, positive as well as negative, strongly reflects the romanticism of that period. It is interesting that audiences of today find Flaherty's documentary films more palatable than the Polynesian feature films. But actually the Van Dyke and Murnau films should be more appealing to anthropologists because they at least allude to real sorts of problems in real sorts of situations. Modern anthropology is much more concerned with the cultural conflicts of *Tabu* than with the reconstructed initiation ceremony of *Moana*.

Cooper and Schoedsack followed *Grass* with a film made in northern Thailand called *Chang* (1927), but, ironically, the most famous scene in the film was the unscripted rampage of a wild elephant through a settlement. Cooper considered *Chang* "our best film" (personal letter to author, 1966). Later

Schoedsack alone made a film called *Rango* (1931) in Sumatra, starring an orangutan. Cooper and Schoedsack went one more step into fantasy to make *King Kong* (1933), shot in Hollywood back lots and studios but set on "Skull Island" off Java, with the "natives" speaking bits of Swahili and Malay, wielding shields of vague New Guinea derivation, and chasing a gorilla-like ape more appropriate to Africa. (The late archaeologist K. C. Chang joked that King Kong was a *Gigantopithecus.*) There is an unexplored parallel between *King Kong* and another fiction film about humans and apes that was released the year before: *Tarzan of the Apes.* Both films grappled with relations between humans and apes; both spawned numerous sequels, remakes, and spin-offs; and each established its hero as a particular prototype of boundary-crosser.

Knud Rasmussen, the Danish-Inuit explorer and ethnographer, collaborated in *Wedding of Palo* (1937), shot in eastern Greenland. Palo's story seems at first suspiciously created by Hollywood but in fact appears to be based on a traditional Eskimo love story. Another film called simply *Eskimo* treats an Inuit love story disrupted by the captain of a trading vessel frozen in the ice near a village. This tradition continues on in the United States with such recent films as the 1974 Inuit story *White Dawn* and in Canada with the first Inuit-made film, *Atanarjuat: The Fast Runner.* Other masterpieces of what might be called ethnographic fiction are Satyajit Ray's *Apu Trilogy* (*Pather Panchali,* 1955; *The Unvanquished,* 1956; and *The World of Apu,* 1959), which follows Apu and his family from boyhood in a Bengal village to university life in Calcutta (see Wood 1971); and the Algerian-French production *Ramparts of Clay* (1969), based on Jean Duvignaud's monograph on a Tunisian village, *Change at Shebika* (1970).

The major strength of the ethnographic fiction film is its ability to focus on peak events of interpersonal relationships and so to explore in detail the dynamics of emotions as they are played out. The danger is that the cultural context may be ethnocentric and shallow. A South African film set among the Ju/'hoansi of the Kalahari, *The Gods Must Be Crazy,* although an international hit, has been criticized by anthropologists on just these grounds (see, e.g., Volkman 1988). And Jack G. Shaheen has written extensively about the overwhelmingly negative images of Arabs on television in the West (1988) and in Hollywood films (2001; see also Hart 2001). Making this sort of film is a great gamble that is rarely attempted and even more rarely won. But the best of the ethnographic fiction films, those that are true to the culture, bring to focus the question we have already touched on: Can fiction create truth? In the next chapter we shall return to this question.

For the third edition of my cultural anthropology textbook, *Seeing Anthropology* (2004), I introduced a feature called "Hollywood-style anthropology," matching each chapter with a fiction feature film or television episode such as *Mr. Baseball, The Milagro Beanfield War, Tampopo, Moonstruck, Pygmalion,* and *Tootsie* to explore anthropological concepts through popular fiction.

BATESON AND MEAD IN BALI AND NEW GUINEA

A decade after Flaherty's first films, ethnography and film were finally brought together by two anthropologists, Gregory Bateson and Margaret Mead. Bateson had done fieldwork among the Iatmul of the Sepik River in northeastern New Guinea and had written a monograph, *Naven* (1936), a complex book with a theoretical sophistication of analysis that has made it a much-admired but little-read masterpiece. Mead had done fieldwork in Samoa and New Guinea, had written numerous monographs and articles, and was already well known for her readable popular ethnographies: *Coming of Age in Samoa* (1928), *Growing Up in New Guinea* (1930a), and *Sex and Temperament in Three Primitive Societies* (1935). Then between 1936 and 1939, Bateson and Mead collaborated in a joint study of children in a Balinese village. The Balinese project made several major contributions to anthropology, but the one that concerns us here was the integration of film and still photography into ethnographic research. As Bateson and Mead wrote in 1942 (p. xii), they used photographs to cover some of the criticisms of their separate earlier work— as a visual filling out of Bateson's impersonalized abstraction and as verifiable documentation for Mead's broad impressionistic descriptions of human behavior. Their research in Bali covered many subjects and was carried out in collaboration with Jane Belo, Colin McPhee, and others then working in Bali. But the focus of Bateson and Mead's research was on the relationship of culture and personality, and particularly on child rearing, which had already been an important theme in Mead's earlier work.

The first book to be published, *Balinese Character* (Bateson and Mead 1942), used a combination of text and still photographs in a way that has rarely been attempted since and has never been surpassed. The movie footage seems to have been less important, or perhaps simply more difficult to shoot, than the still photographs. In any case, Bateson and Mead eventually used the stills in their major publication on Bali (1942), and the films were finished a decade later under the supervision of Mead alone. The entire project warrants much more consideration and thought than it has received.

But here I want to talk only about the films. In addition to the 25,000 still photographs that were culled for the two Bali books (Bateson and Mead 1942; Mead and MacGregor 1951), Bateson shot 22,000 feet of 16 mm movie film. From this, six films were edited and released in 1950. These films are ethnographic in the most literal sense of the word. Like written ethnographies, they describe behavior and present the results of the ethnographic study. For the most part, they focus on children interacting with each other and with adults. For example, they try to show visually the Balinese practice of stimulating an infant nearly to the point of climax and then suddenly breaking off contact. Bateson, especially, argued (1949) that this pattern is important in contributing to the nonclimaxing "steady state" of adult Balinese, and it has visual manifestations that can be shown well in film.

Two features of the Bateson and Mead series are particularly noteworthy. One film is a longitudinal study of a single boy, Karba, from seven months to thirty-four months of age, following him through the crucial developmental stages of early childhood. In *Childhood Rivalry in Bali and New Guinea*, the Balinese behavior is set off against the very different behavior of another culture, the Iatmul, whom Bateson had studied between 1929 and 1933 and whom the two revisited for eight months in the middle of their Balinese research.

The Bateson and Mead research was the first to try systematically to work out the implications of using film as an integral part of anthropological research and reportage, a problem treated in most of the next chapter. In a written ethnography, it seems easy (because we are accustomed to do so) to use words to describe critical moments and practices, to describe the development of a child through phases, and to set the behavior of a particular culture into a cross-cultural context. Bateson and Mead did this in print, in their two Bali books. They also used film, not to do just the same thing but to achieve the same ends. They deliberately used film to show visual movement and holistic interrelationships of complex scenes that could be much better presented on film than described purely in words. Thus, their use of film was planned to be integrated fully with, and supplementary to, the written ethnography.

Another major contribution was Bateson and Mead's concern with spelling out the circumstances of their photography. In the book *Balinese Character* (1942), Bateson contributed a chapter (pp. 49–54) in which he explicitly discusses the question of Balinese camera consciousness and suggests factors that diminish its influence; distinguishes between posed photographs and photographs taken in contexts the anthropologists created, for example, by paying for a dance; describes the various sorts of selections in the original shooting and final editing; mentions the matter of retouching photographs; and explains various technological factors. Elsewhere, Mead (1970) emphasized the importance of laying out these same basic facts. But on the whole, even this minimal prerequisite for scientific credibility has not been repeated.

There are problems in the Balinese films. Some are purely technical. In the 1930s, Bateson was limited to a clumsy, tripod-based camera without synchronous sound and to relatively short takes. And because of financial concern, he shot most of his footage at 16 frames per second (fps). When the film was edited, it included Mead's narration and was intended to be projected at 24 instead of 16 fps. The irony is obvious. This filmic report, which is so concerned with natural movement and pace of life, shows the Balinese moving at a pace 50 percent faster than normal. (It seems to have been a matter of faith among film people that the faster speed—"sound speed"—was essential to high-quality sound. In fact, if the Balinese films are projected at the speed at which they were shot, 16 fps, Mead's voice drops an octave or so but is still understandable, and the Balinese pace can be appreciated. However, this is not always feasible. Most film projectors do not have 16 fps capability or else have an automatic sound switch-off at that speed.) Fortunately, most of the footage used in *Trance and Dance in Bali* seems to have been shot originally at 24 fps.

A more serious problem in the Balinese films is that the action on the screen often does not show clearly what the narration claims. This may be in part a result of the way the footage was originally conceived. It is not really clear to what extent the footage was intended to illustrate the ethnographic understandings. Neither ethnographer has written much about this aspect of their research. But in one passage Bateson writes that "we treated the cameras in the field as recording instruments, not as devices for illustrating our theses" (Bateson and Mead 1942, 49). This is rather ambiguous. The final ethnographic reports, like the films, were written to prove their theses. That is, selections from the data and from the footage were made, and the final results were interpretive. And I certainly would not now want to defend the position that "objective" footage is desirable or even possible. I understand it to mean that because the footage was shot as the research proceeded, some understandings of Balinese culture were reached only when it was too late to capture them on film.

The Bateson and Mead ethnographic films represent a major advance in concept, even if that concept could not be fully realized. But, like Flaherty's films, they have had little real effect. It is frustrating to speculate how much more advanced ethnographic films might now be if the Bateson and Mead innovations in the visual field had been widely understood and built on in the 1940s and 1950s.

It was only after World War II that ethnographic film came into its own. Four filmmakers played central roles in this development: Jean Rouch in France and John Marshall, Robert Gardner, and Timothy Asch in America.

All are men, all had studied anthropology, none had any formal training in cinematography, all collaborated with other anthropologists, all have inspired others but none (except Rouch) have really founded a school of pupils carrying on their work, all were active through most of the second half of the twentieth century, and all knew each other and interacted over the decades. They differed in even more ways. They never formed a single movement or school of ethnographic filmmaking, but taken together, they formed ethnographic film.

JEAN ROUCH

Before the Second World War, Jean Rouch had begun studying engineering and then, during the German occupation of France, had been sent to West Africa, where he built roads. He met Damoure Zika, who would collaborate with him on many films and star in *Jaguar* and who was in the car accident that killed Rouch in West Africa in 2004. But it was in those early wartime days that Rouch determined to become an anthropologist and to make films (see Lucien Taylor's interview with Rouch in Taylor 2002, 129–146).

Over the years since 1946, Rouch made dozens of films, mainly in West Africa, focusing on the Songhay and the Dogon (see the definitive—up to 1999—filmography in Rouch 2003, 345–382). In just a few years around 1960 he made four films that are of extreme importance. One of these films that had not been made in West Africa had the greatest influence on other filmmakers.

In 1960, Jean Rouch was working with Edgar Morin, a sociologist, on *Chronicle of a Summer* (1961). Using the newest portable 16 mm cameras and synchronous sound equipment, Rouch and Morin enlisted several cameramen to help explore the state of mind of people in Paris in a summer when the Algerian War dominated life. They made no pretense of using omniscient invisible cameras. One or both of the filmmakers often appeared onscreen, asking questions or participating in discussions. When the bulk of the film had been edited, the rough cut was screened for the participants. Their reactions to themselves and to the other participants and their evaluations of the truth or falseness of the various scenes were being filmed. This formed the second section of the film. The final section was a sequence that followed Rouch and Morin as they paced the halls of the Musée de l'Homme, evaluating their own film (see especially Rouch 2003, 229–342).

The reality captured by the new synchronous sound, and by the deliberate intrusion of the filmmakers, had a profound effect on French filmmakers like Truffaut and Godard. Rouch is considered a father of French cinema verité, but he had little immediate effect on ethnographic film in the United States. Most ethnographic filmmakers have tried to create the illusion of the ethnographic present, without anthropologist. The possibilities of Rouch's approach are important. It is not just a matter of showing the anthropologist in a scene or two but of building the films around the inescapable fact that an anthropologist and a filmmaker are on the spot and are interacting with the people and thus influencing behavior.

Likewise, Rouch's technique of showing people reacting to their own images has rarely been followed up in any systematic way. Altogether, by showing behavior, showing how it was filmed, and then chewing over its meaning, *Chronicle of a Summer* achieves a remarkable closure totally lacking in most ethnographic films.

The earliest film of these four, *Les maîtres fous* (1955), focuses on the Hauka, a possession ritual carried out by Songhay workers who had come from Mali to Accra, then the capital of the British colony of the Gold Coast. The film opens with shots of the workers in the streets of Accra. Then it follows them through the possession ceremony and finally takes them back again to their labor in Accra, with flashback cuts to remind us visually of the same men who play such different roles. For example, the man who acted the general in the ceremony also acts an army private in Accra. There is a heavy narration, but it directly complements the visuals. That is, it does not just fill in vaguely relevant or background information, but it explains the wild behavior of the ceremony and also gives an interpretation of the ceremony as a mocking reenactment of the attitudes and rituals of the British colonial officers. The title ambiguously refers to the "mad masters"—the British colonials—or the "masters of madness," the Hauka performers themselves. Finally, the narration proposes a psychological explanation, suggesting that the ritual has a cathartic effect, allowing the natives to mock the British on Sunday so that they can sanely submit to colonial servitude during the week.

Les maîtres fous is a powerful and controversial film; perhaps its power and its controversy stem from similar features. More than in most ethnographic films, its visuals and its sounds focus, rather than dissipate, the viewers' attention. The Hauka performers are a disturbing sight: men in trance, seemingly out of control, frothing at the mouth and drinking dog's blood. The film does not try to gloss over or pretty up that image. It forces the viewer to observe reality and then leads the viewer into deeper understanding. The film is at the opposite extreme from the banality of those travelogues that show all people, however exotic, the same. *Les maîtres fous* says that these men are very different from us, and we must understand why. One of Jean Rouch's favorite admonitions to ethnographic filmmakers is "Tell a story!"

The Lion Hunters was filmed in the upper Niger area over a period of years (1957–1964). It follows the Gow, a group of Songhay who are called in by Fulani pastoralists to kill some lions that are raiding their herds. Where Rouch in *Les maîtres fous* developed a theory of catharsis to explain the Hauka ritual, here in *The Lion Hunters* he draws on the symbolic structuralism of Claude Lévi-Strauss, whose theories dominated anthropology at the time. Thus, the village of the Fulani was opposed to the bush of the lions. When the lions crossed over to the village, they had broken the cosmic contract and had to be removed by the rituals of the Gow. Paul Stoller (1992, 118ff) has emphasized how important and powerful the words are in this film. The incantations give the poisons and traps and bows and arrows their potency. The Gow rituals are a comprehensive collection of imitative magic, sympathetic magic, and pattern number magic, all playing on the village-bush duality.

We are aware of Rouch himself in *The Lion Hunters*. He never appears in frame, as he and Moran do in *Chronicle of a Summer,* but we ride along with him in his Land Rover into the bush, farther than far; he acknowledges dropping the camera when a trapped lion charges; and we read the telegram summoning him back to Africa when the lions resume their marauding.

Jaguar, which Rouch worked on over the same period (1957–1967), is yet a different cinematic experiment. "Jaguars" are the young men of the upper Niger who in those days made the long trek south to the Gold Coast (now part of Ghana) to see the world, have adventures, make money, and come home with great gifts for their friends and greater stories. Rouch had written extensively (e.g., 1956) about the pattern of migration, but he looked for some way to show it on film. Paul Stoller, who also worked with the Songhay, wrote a novel about jaguars coming to the United States (1999). But Rouch and Damoure Zika made a film. Zika and two friends played the jaguars who walked to Accra, with Rouch filming them. In its spontaneous good humor, it is like something the Beatles might have made. In an interview with John Marshall and John Adams, Rouch said: "A film like *Jaguar* was fun. It was shot as a silent film and we made it up as we went along. It's a kind of journal de route—my working journal along the way with my camera. We were playing a game together" (2003, 205). Then, two years later, Rouch brought back a print, virtually unedited, to show to the three jaguars. They found a studio and in one day the three of them improvised a sound track of what they thought they remembered saying and thinking. It was fun.

In his great spurt of creativity that produced these four films, Rouch explored most of the important themes that we shall be discussing: ethnographic fact- and theory-based film, collaboration with subjects, and incorporating subjects' feedback, documentation, and fiction.

Rouch is now quite accessible in English. Paul Stoller, an American anthropologist, has done extensive research over the years on the Songhay. His book *The Cinematic Griot* (1992) is a particularly insightful analysis of Rouch's ethnography and cinema on the Songhay. Steven Feld, another American anthropologist, has interviewed Rouch several times and recently edited and translated *Ciné-ethnography* (Rouch 2003), a major collection of articles by and about Rouch, including an extended treatment of *Chronicle of a Summer*. The March 2005 issue of the *American Anthropologist* included "Cine-trance: A Tribute to Jean Rouch (1917–2004)," a series of short articles edited by Jeff Himpele and Faye Ginsburg.

JOHN MARSHALL

For the two decades after Bateson and Mead's Balinese expedition, the ethnographic film scene was quiescent. The Second World War had intervened, of course, diverting personnel and resources and closing down field opportunities. It was not until the 1950s that ethnographic film began to flourish again. When it did, an extraordinary amount of the crucial activity was based in and around Harvard University and was carried out by three men who had all worked together at one time or another.

What might be called the Harvard movement really started outside academia with the Marshall family expeditions to the Kalahari. Beginning in 1951, Laurence K. Marshall, a retired businessman, led a series of expeditions into the Kalahari Desert of southern Africa to study the Bushmen. Although the Marshall expeditions included scientists of various sorts, their core was always Marshall and his family: his wife, Lorna, and his two children, Elizabeth and John. It was planned that Lorna Marshall would make ethnographic studies of the Bushmen, John would make films, and Elizabeth, who had a flair for writing, would write a book. Fortunately no anthropologist was around to tell them how unfeasible it all was. The results were outstanding. George Peter Murdock has referred to "ethnographic accounts of outstanding quality . . . by . . . housewives like Lorna Marshall" (1972, 18). Elizabeth Marshall Thomas's book *The Harmless People* (1959) has become a classic popular account, and John Marshall's films have played a major role in the development of ethnographic film.

By 1954, John Marshall had shot hundreds of thousands of feet of film on the Bushmen. About this time, the Marshalls contacted J. O. Brew, then director of the Peabody Museum at Harvard. Brew recognized the value of the Marshall footage and invited the family to collaborate with Harvard. The

Film Study Center was established in the basement of the Peabody Museum, and a graduate student in the Anthropology Department at Harvard, Robert Gardner, was chosen to be its director.

The Hunters was finished in 1956 and released in 1958. It quickly became a most popular and respected ethnographic film. In many ways it was pure Flaherty. Based on long but nonprofessional study of a people, it followed four individuals through a major man-against-nature crisis, the hunt for meat, which culminated in the killing of a giraffe.

The film can be criticized on a number of grounds. It tells a story, but a story that was composed in the editing room with footage shot not over a single two-week period but on expeditions that took place over several years. There are some inconsistencies that bother the fastidious viewer: the four hunters are not always the same people; stock giraffe footage is edited in omnisciently while the hunters are still searching for it. (However, the persistent rumor that the giraffe was finished off with a rifle is not true.)

The most serious problem with *The Hunters* today is that its basic premise is inaccurate, as John Marshall was later to recognize. In the mid-1950s, when the film was made, the best anthropological opinion held that hunting-and-gathering groups like the Bushmen were hanging on to a marginal environment with an inadequate subsistence technology. This was at least partially the result of the way fieldwork had been done. For example, the Marshall expedition, appearing in a Bushman camp with its trucks loaded with food and water (Thomas 1959, 5–6), certainly must have tempted the Bushmen to exaggerate their subsistence problems. And there would have been little reason for the Marshalls to doubt what they were told by both Bushmen and anthropologists. But then, in the early 1960s, anthropologists like Richard Lee worked among hunter-gatherers, accompanying the people without the benefit of Land Rovers and masses of supplies, making careful studies of what the Bushmen actually ate. Lee showed that the Bushmen actually had an abundance of food—especially in the undramatic but protein-packed mongongo nuts, which were available by the millions. Equally careful ethnography elsewhere contributed to revised versions of other foraging groups. The publication of *Man the Hunter* (Lee and De Vore 1968) marked the acceptance of a new understanding of hunting-and-gathering peoples. It also meant that the major premise of *The Hunters* (that the Bushmen were starving) could no longer be accepted. But although the film is ethnographically faulty on the role of hunting in Bushman life, its portrayal of the local knowledge involved in hunting itself remains unimpeached.

The Hunters did not really represent a conceptual advance beyond Flaherty or Bateson and Mead. As a film, it was better than Flaherty's. The account of Bushman hunting was more systematic, and throughout the narration Marshall tried to penetrate the Bushmen's minds more deeply. He was less the outsider and idyll creator than Flaherty had been. One of its greatest virtues was that *The Hunters* was modern. By the 1950s the earlier films had become dated. They were valued and enjoyed, but not unlike the way in which Charlie Chaplin's films are enjoyed. *The Hunters* was proof that fine ethnographic films could still be made.

After their collaboration on *The Hunters,* Marshall and Gardner had gone their separate ways. Marshall was banned from the Kalahari by the South African government for twenty years, 1958–1978. He turned to subjects at home. He shot *Titicut Follies* (1968), a powerful view of the State Prison for the Criminally Insane in Bridgewater, Massachusetts, for Frederick Wiseman. (Wiseman later produced an important series of films on American institutions like *High School, Basic Training, Hospital, Law and Order,* and *Juvenile Court.*) Marshall went alone to Pittsburgh, where he made a series of police films.

But Marshall's extensive Bushman footage was too important to lie idle. In the mid-1960s, work resumed on it. Others active in Marshall's new Bushman effort were Lorna Marshall, film editor Frank Galvin, and Timothy Asch. Asch had studied still photography under Edward Weston and Minor White and had done graduate work in anthropology at Harvard and Boston universities.

Asch and the Marshalls set up a large ethnographic film studio in Somerville, Massachusetts (near Cambridge), under the title of Documentary Educational Resources (DER). This became an extraordinarily productive center during the late 1960s and the early 1970s. Here the Asch-Marshall group edited nearly twenty more Bushman films, each a short film on a single subject. The first was *N/um Tchai* (1966), about the Bushman trance ceremony. The footage, of course, had been shot ten years earlier. And although the ceremony is usually done at night, the Bushmen performed it at dawn when it could be filmed. Wild sound and narration were added.

The editors made an innovative solution to the constant problem of how to make a complex event understandable without resorting to a wordy explanatory narrative. They decided to show the ceremony twice. The first time an explanatory narration was read over still photographs of the action, while the second part of the film just ran the footage of the ceremony with well-synchronized wild sound but without any narration.

Another film in the new Bushman series, *An Argument about a Marriage,* also used this technique. The film shows a complex and heated argument between two groups of Bushmen that had arisen when a woman, who had been deserted by her husband and had married again, was reunited with her first husband and the various people involved tried to sort out their rights and duties. The first part of the film introduces the participants in still photographs, while the narration tries to explain and unravel the argument. The second part of the film retraces the quarrel, with wild sound—actually the dialogue—added later. A few English subtitles are used in the second half of the film so that the audience can keep up with the argument.

But even with the preliminary explanation and the subtitles, it is almost impossible for most viewers to follow the argument, certainly on the first viewing. The trance ceremony in *N/um Tchai* is understandable through this approach. But "an argument about marriage" is one of the most difficult subjects for film. Film can easily show how Bushmen argue but not so easily explain the argument itself. Marriage itself is a complex, symbolically charged event; the argument about marriage is an abstract wordy examination of its implications. In order for audiences to really understand *An Argument,* a written companion that can add background details, kinship diagrams, and the like is necessary. In 1974, DER began to distribute study guides for *N/um Tchai* and the studio's other films (L. Marshall and Biesele 1974; Reichlin 1974a–g; Reichlin and Marshall 1974). Previously, printed material had accompanied films only as an occasional extraordinary event, and it was usually only an inadequate page or two. DER took a major step in making the production of an adequate study guide accompaniment a routine part of ethnographic filmmaking.

An Argument about a Marriage and some of the other new Bushman films deliberately pushed the limits of film's ability to deal with complex social behavior. Spearing a seal, hunting a giraffe, or building a house are all much more visual, and thus much more amenable to filmic treatment, than is an argument about a marriage. Most ethnographic films have concentrated on the visual technology. But although the study of material culture (or the material aspects of culture) was a major part of early ethnography, now most ethnologists spend most of their thought on more complex and nonvisual events like arguments about marriages. The Marshall group, and particularly Timothy Asch, made a rare attempt to use ethnographic film to treat the major concerns of anthropology today.

When Marshall was allowed to return to the Kalahari in 1978, life had changed drastically for the Ju/'hoansi. Marshall made no attempt to re-create the "untouched" scenes he had filmed in the 1950s. Instead he made *!Nai, the Story of a !Kung Woman.* Bateson and Mead had made *Karba's First Years,* incorporating footage of a little Balinese boy shot over a period of three years. This was the first longitudinal ethnographic film. But Marshall took this one step further. He used footage of !Nai from her childhood in the 1950s and sync sound footage from the late 1970s. A narration (in English translation) of !Nai telling the story of her life bridges the two sets of footage. She remembers her idyllic girlhood and her tempestuous prepuberty marriage, and we see her current life in a South African detention camp, living on rations. She is paid money to be photographed, but the old sharing system has broken down and her wealth is resented by other Ju/'hoansi. Men are being recruited by the South African army to fight guerrillas. And another film crew is on location shooting what will be *The Gods Must Be Crazy.*

Marshall spent much of the last twenty-five years of the twentieth century in the Kalahari, devoting himself to the Ju/'hoansi. His last film was the six-hour *A Kalahari Family,* truly his magnum opus. It is the story of families in the Kalahari—his own American family and the Ju/'hoansi families they knew. Toward the end it becomes increasingly argumentative as Marshall presents his own understanding of what has happened and what is best for the Ju/'hoansi. A collection of essays by and about Marshall's work was published in 1993, as he was working on this last film (Ruby, 1993). And extended considerations of *A Kalahari Family* by seven anthropologists appeared in the *Visual Anthropology Review* in 2003 (vol. 19, nos. 1–2).

ROBERT GARDNER

In the early 1950s, while Robert Gardner was a graduate student at the University of Washington, he founded and ran a small documentary film company called Orbit Films. With Bill Heick as cameraman, Orbit produced two ethnographic films on the Kwakiutl of British Columbia: *Blunden Harbor* and *Dances of the Kwakiutl.* When he was at Harvard with the Film Study Center, Gardner returned to ethnographic film. He accompanied the Marshalls to the Kalahari in 1955 and then played some small role in the editing of a portion of the Bushman footage into a film called *The Hunters.*

After working with John Marshall on *The Hunters,* Gardner began making plans for another large expedition. In 1961 he organized the Harvard Peabody Expedition, which studied the Dani, in what was then Netherlands New Guinea (and subsequently the Indonesian province called serially Irian Barat, Irian Jaya, and Papua). Although these Dani had been first reported in 1938 by an expedition from the American Museum of Natural History and were not "unknown" or "untouched" when the Harvard expedition arrived, many Dani were still using stone axes and carrying on warfare with bows and arrows and spears. It was one of the rare chances for anthropologists to observe firsthand these sorts of activities. The standard pattern for ethnography has been for a single ethnographer to work alone and report a single point of view; or if two ethnographers work together, the results are reported in joint publications as consensus conclusions (e.g., if Bateson and Mead differed in their conclusions about Bali, we have no hint of it in print). The Harvard Peabody Expedition is practically unique in that it resulted in a number of books, articles, and films by different people (including myself) with different views of the same Dani doing the same things.

Gardner's film *Dead Birds* was shot during the first five months of the expedition. Gardner worked closely with Jan Broekhuijse, a Dutch-government anthropologist who had studied the Dani; he also used input from the rest of the expedition; and, of course, he was a trained anthropologist himself. In the summer of 1962, midway through the editing of *Dead Birds,* he made a return visit to New Guinea and discussed the film with me; and at the end of 1963, after I had been with the Dani for eighteen months, I returned to Cambridge to help with the final editing of the film.

Dead Birds is, like *The Hunters,* still very much in the Flaherty tradition. It is a long, inclusive film following Weyak the warrior and Pua the little swineherd as the group moves through a series of war crises. The major events are not reconstructed or staged. Battles and funerals were going on during the filming and are shown in the film as they happened. (The persistent rumors that the Harvard Peabody Expedition instigated or encouraged warfare are untrue. We did, of course, observe warfare, and we did not attempt to discourage it. See K. Heider 1997a, 19, 181.) Gardner's interpretation of the meaning of war to the Dani or his attributions of thoughts to specific people at specific times can be challenged. For example, I doubt that the Dani are as explicitly philosophical about death as Gardner states (see K. Heider 1970, 138–140). But our disagreements fall well within the range of acceptable variation in ethnographic interpretation.

Inevitably the film is incomplete as a definitive description of Dani warfare. For example, it was made at the beginning of a long ethnographic study, and not until my third trip to the Dani, in 1968, did I learn the details of another phase of Dani warfare, quite different from the ritual phase shown in *Dead Birds* (see K. Heider 1970, 1972a).

But if *Dead Birds* is Flaherty-like in some aspects, Gardner's concept of film tied to ethnographic research owes much to Bateson and Mead. This was not a "film expedition"; it was an ethnographic expedition that coordinated the efforts of three ethnographers (Broekhuijse, Gardner, and Heider), a natural historian and novelist (Peter Matthiessen), a botanist (Chris Versteegh), a professional still photographer (Eliot Elisofon), and others (Michael Rockefeller and Samuel Putnam), as well as, in the 1968 and 1970 follow-ups, a psychologist (Eleanor Rosch) (see also K. Heider 2001–2002).

Dead Birds is only one of the Harvard Peabody Expedition reports on the Dani. The film is also tied into the written ethnographic reports through a lengthy ethnographic companion, or study guide. This describes the ethnography of the Dani vis-à-vis the film and includes Gardner's statement about the making of the film, together with a shot-by-shot analysis of the film keyed to the narration (K. Heider 1972a). More recently Gardner has released a DVD with much additional materials about *Dead Birds,* including Jean Rouch's French narration. Thus, not only is *Dead Birds* a dramatic eighty-three-minute account of the Dani, but it is also usable as a thoroughly documented study film.

Dead Birds was in many ways a watershed for ethnographic film. It was made without synchronous sound. In 1960, when the equipment for the expedition was being bought, synchronous sound in New Guinea was still a fantasy. By the mid-1960s, reliable portable synchronous sound equipment was available. Before *Dead Birds,* there was a mere handful of films that could be called ethnography; in the decades since *Dead Birds,* thousands have been made.

As *Dead Birds* was being finished, Gardner moved the Film Study Center from the Peabody Museum to Harvard's new Visual Arts Center, where he had at last a major training and production laboratory. During the next years he assisted many people in shooting or editing ethnographic films, and he taught courses in ethnographic films. But, unfortunately, the promise of real cooperation between the Film Study Center and Harvard's Anthropology Department never materialized, and a great opportunity to develop the concepts and practice of ethnographic film was lost.

In the late 1960s, Gardner organized a new ethnographic film project on nomads. After continual frustration in finding a suitable location, he filmed the Afar and the Hamar of Ethiopia. The first of these films, *Rivers of Sand,* was released in 1974. Meanwhile, when in Ethiopia, he learned of a group of Nuer in Ethiopia and persuaded Hilary Harris to make a film of them.

The Nuer is a film of images of the incredibly tall, thin Nuer and their cattle. Through Evans-Pritchard's ethnographic writings, the Nuer have become one of the "standard," best-known cultures in anthropological literature. Hilary Harris is a professional filmmaker who has been especially interested in filming modern dance and ballet. This interest shows plainly in *The Nuer.* The film could be titled "The Dance of the Cattle." It is one of the most visually beautiful films ever made, and it shows the rhythm and pace of Nuer life, which no ethnographer could ever capture in words (although it is instructive to compare the film with chapter 1, "Interest in Cattle," of Evans-Pritchard's 1940 book). But its principles are cinema aesthetic: its framing, cutting, and juxtaposition of images are done with little regard for ethnographic reality.

There is one important step forward: while Harris and his assistant, George Breidenbach, were on location, Gardner visited them and shot some scenes in synchronous sound. In the finished film we see an old man evidently responding to questions, describing in the Nuer language what is important to him, especially his cattle. Gardner has been criticized for the *Dead Birds* narration, in which he says what the Dani characters are thinking. Although the thoughts on the whole seemed reasonable to me, it is obvious that they strike U.S. audiences as poetic fiction. Now, with synchronous sound, Gardner is able to let the Nuer speak for themselves (always presuming that the audience will accept the validity of the English translation that follows).

But even if *The Nuer* is ethnographically shallow, it has real use in teaching anthropology. It can give students a general holistic feeling for the people, their cattle, and their environment, helping them build a kind of cognitive landscape into which they can place Evans-Pritchard's written descriptions of Nuer social organization and ritual.

Robert Gardner's first Ethiopian film, *Rivers of Sand* (1974), is about the Hamar people. In this film, Gardner takes the synchronous sound interview technique a step beyond *The Nuer* and builds the entire film around a Hamar woman who sits, relaxed, before the camera and speaks at great length about her life. She is particularly introspective about her own culture, and so she makes an ideal interpreter for us. Between shots of the woman talking, Gardner uses sequences of Hamar life that more or less directly illustrate what she has said.

A second important feature of *Rivers of Sand* is the ambitiousness of its subject matter. It attempts to describe the role of women in Hamar society. This seems like a particularly nonvisual subject. It is a matter of moods and attitudes and cultural norms, and not nearly as directly behavioral as housebuilding or farming or warfare. Yet Gardner takes on the challenge, crisscrossing back and forth over the subject, building up a sense of it through the visual images and through his narration and through the Hamar woman's words. It is a film without a plotline, and so it often is repetitious. It sometimes takes symbolic leaps, as when the images cut from a girl's neck iron to the branding of a cow's neck. And it retains the ambiguity of reality, as when we are told of the pain of whipping but then see a girl smile as she undergoes it. It is not an easy film to watch or to understand. But Gardner has attempted to move ethnographic film closer to the real concerns of anthropology. That is, more anthropologists are concerned with describing cultural attitudes and values than are trying to describe warfare or housebuilding.

In the mid-1980s, Gardner made his most complex and difficult film, *Forest of Bliss* (1986). It explores death and dying in Benares, the most sacred spot on Hindu India's most sacred river, the Ganges. There is no narration, no subtitling, and the richly allusive visuals are not edited in actual narrative sequence. Many viewers were lost, and even those who followed the general themes missed much of the rich symbolism. The film triggered a raucous attack (see Ruby 2000, 110–113). Ákos Östör, who was the main anthropological consultant on the project, published an article explaining the ethnography behind the film (1994). In 1987, two years after the film was finished, Gardner and Östör recorded a scene-by-scene discussion about their intentions and understandings. A German version of this conversation was published two years later (Gardner and Östör 1989), and in 2001 the expanded conversation was published as a book titled *Making "Forest of Bliss": Intention, Circumstance, and Chance in Nonfiction Film* (Gardner and Östör 2001).

I know of no other instance where the filmmakers have revealed so much in depth and in detail of their "intentions, circumstances, and chances." We learn the extent to which Gardner has loaded into the film symbols from the Hindu ritual and also from Greek mythology and how he expects the viewer to see and retain information that can only later be meaningfully conceptualized. We hear Gardner and Östör laying out some of their disagreements about, for example, the meaning of the far shore of the Ganges across from the cremation steps of Benares. To work through the film with book in hand is to gain a unique insight into this originally very private composition of Gardner's. Of course, such revelation is risky. Much of the criticism of Gardner's film has been based on what he revealed about himself in print, not in the films themselves (e.g., Ruby 2000, 95–113). His next book (2006) is sure to be even more revealing.

TIMOTHY ASCH

It was an impressive testimony to the insight and thoroughness of John Marshall's photography that the footage he shot in the 1950s could be so effectively edited into the films of the 1970s, when he collaborated with Timothy Asch. Much of the inspiration for these shorter films came from Asch. He had studied anthropology and still photography and had collaborated with Marshall's sister, Elizabeth Marshall (Thomas), on her project in West Africa. Asch was teaching anthropology at Brandeis and Harvard, and throughout his career he was committed to exploring ways to make films that would enhance teaching. Films like *An Argument about a Marriage, N/um Tchai,* and *A Joking Relationship* were particularly designed for classroom use.

The next step was taken in 1968, when Asch began a collaboration with Napoleon Chagnon. Chagnon had spent nineteen months on an ethnographic study of the Yanomamö in southern Venezuela. He returned to the United States, wrote up his materials for publication (e.g., 1997), and then, after having digested his understanding of the Yanomamö, returned with Asch to make films. The two were well matched: Asch, the filmmaker with training in anthropology; and Chagnon, the anthropologist who knew the culture and had experience with cinematography (during his earlier trips he had shot very creditable footage on the Yanomamö). And they were able to use synchronous sound equipment. In the summer of 1968, they shot footage for *The Feast,* a twenty-nine-minute film on intervillage feasting, an important feature of Yanomamö life that Chagnon had described and analyzed in chapter 4 of his Yanomamö monograph (1997, 105–117).

The Feast uses the same twofold approach that Asch had developed for *N/um Tchai* and *An Argument about a Marriage*: an introductory section, with stills in which the narration describes background and events of a particular feast, followed by the running film of the feast with English subtitles, which translate statements in the synchronous sound discussion and arguments that take place as the visitors arrive and visitors and hosts discuss gifts and counter-gifts.

Two years later Asch and Chagnon again collaborated, this time in a much more ambitious project: to make short films from the Yanomamö materials that would illustrate the wide range of topics covered in introductory anthropology courses, from subsistence activities to mythology. There were many problems in the collaboration, which Asch has described with unusual frankness (1972). It is a revealing cautionary tale of how even well-conceived ethnographic film projects can be affected by the myriad frustrations of using sophisticated equipment in remote jungles, problems of rapport, and personality differences. In all, they shot some 78,000 feet of film and worked this corpus into more than forty films. Among of the most important of these were *The Ax Fight* and *A Man Called "Bee."* Later, Peter Biella, Gary Seaman, and Chagnon (1997) developed an interactive disc of *The Ax Fight,* designed to allow students to stop the film and pull up genealogical information on the people involved in the action.

After working with Chagnon on the Yanomamö films, Asch shot footage in Afghanistan with anthropologist Asen Balikci, out of which came *Sons of Haji Omar.* And now Asch was working in the field with his wife, Patsy

Asch, who would become an increasingly important partner in his subsequent films.

From 1976 to 1982 the Asches were based at the Australian National University in Canberra, from which they made important films in Indonesia. They collaborated with James Fox on two films on the Indonesian island of Roti—*Water of Words* (1983) and *Spear and Sword* (1989)—and with E. D. Lewis on *A Celebration of Origins* (1993).

The major project of their Australian years was a collaboration with Linda Connor, an anthropologist who had been studying trance and ritual in Bali. In all, they produced five films: *A Balinese Trance Séance* (1979), following a trance performance of Jero Tapakan, a spirit medium; *Jero on Jero: A Balinese Trance Séance Observed* (1981), in which Linda Connor and Jero Tapakan watched and commented on the first film; *The Medium Is the Masseuse* (1981), where we see Jero Tapakan in her other profession as a masseuse; *Jero Tapakan: Stories from the Life of a Balinese Healer* (1991), where Jero tells her life story; and *Releasing the Spirits: A Village Cremation in Bali* (1991), in which a village performs a large cremation ceremony for all those who have died in recent years. Jero is present and unexpectedly goes into trance, speaking as a spirit medium. Connor and the Asches published *Jero Tapakan, Balinese Healer: An Ethnographic Film Monograph* (1986; revised edition, 1996), which included essays on the filming and on the ethnography of Balinese trance, as well as shot-by-shot lists for each of the first of four films.

This Balinese package represents the culmination of Asch's work, and indeed of the main themes in ethnographic filmmaking: multiple short films made in close collaboration with a knowledgeable anthropologist, showing the reaction of the main character to the filming, and including the outside team onscreen, all supported and enhanced by printed matter to make the film accessible to students and experts alike. In addition, we have a superb volume on Asch's life and work edited by E. D. Lewis (2004) and written by many of Asch's colleagues (see also Henley 2005 and Elder 2001–2002). An earlier collection of articles and photographs of Asch, with some overlap with the Lewis volume, appeared in *Visual Anthropology Review* in 1995 (vol. 11, no. 1), under the editorship of Nancy Lutkehaus.

This has not pretended to be an exhaustive account of all ethnographic films. Yet these four—Rouch, Marshall, Gardner, and Asch—have been the dominant figures in the second half of the twentieth century. Other writers have focused on other contributors: David and Judith MacDougall (see Grimshaw 2001 and MacDougall 1998) and Melissa Llewelyn-Davies (see Grimshaw 2001). Many others who have only begun their careers will tell the story of ethnographic film in the twenty-first century.

There are a few other projects that should be mentioned.

UNIVERSITY OF CALIFORNIA
AMERICAN INDIAN SERIES

Most ethnographic filmmaking involves some influence of behavior by film-makers in the interest of the ethnographic present. For instance, we decided during the filming of *Dead Birds* not to give the Dani red cloth or steel axes as trade goods, and Gardner deliberately avoided showing members of the expedition in the film.

But, on occasion, filmmakers have done a wholesale re-creation of events. In the 1920s, both Flaherty and the ethnographic fiction films did this. In the 1950s, Samuel A. Barrett, an anthropologist with the Department of Anthropology at the University of California, Berkeley, made a series of films on California Indians (Barrett 1961). The subjects were asked to reenact such old traits as leaching acorns or making a sinew-backed bow. As it happens, some of the most important footage was shot as a spin-off of this project—a two-night curing ceremony performed by a Pomo shaman, Essie Parrish. Two films of the second night have been released (*Sucking Doctor* and its short version, *Pomo Shaman*), but funds ran out before footage of the first night could be edited.

THE NETSILIK ESKIMO PROJECT

The most ambitious film reconstruction project ever mounted was focused on the Netsilik Eskimos of Pelly Bay, Canada. When the Soviets launched their Sputnik in 1958, the United States was shocked into awareness that it was lagging behind in the hard sciences. Government funds were poured into a crash program designed to improve the teaching of science at all levels. But within a few years social scientists began to be concerned that their fields were being neglected. One result was the establishment of Educational Services Inc. (ESI)—which later became the Educational Development Center—in Cambridge, drawing on Harvard and MIT intellectual resources and funded by the National Science Foundation. It was decided that the social sciences could best be represented in the primary grades by anthropology, using the exoticism of other cultures to convey basic concepts. A number of curriculum units were planned, all using carefully designed films. During the early 1960s, ESI contracted for numerous film projects in Iraq, Mexico, New Guinea, Kenya, and Canada.

The only unit that was successfully completed was the one on the Netsilik Eskimos, emphasizing ecological adaptation to an extreme environment. The Netsilik series was produced by Quentin Brown and two anthropologists, Asen Balikci and Guy Mary-Rousseliere, worked closely with the camera crews in the field (see Hockings 2001–2002). An ethnographic present of 1919 was used. The Netsilik who worked on the project re-created the clothing and houses and subsistence activities in use forty years earlier, drawing on their own memories and the report of anthropologist Knud Rasmussen, who had visited the area in 1923 (Balikci and Brown 1966). Nine 30-minute films were produced. Each was a thorough view of a set of activities associated with a particular season, such as operating a fishing weir or hunting caribou. The films have excellently dubbed natural sound but no narration or even subtitles. They were designed as part of an inclusive educational package and are accompanied by teachers' manuals, student exercise books, and the like. The films are intentionally close to raw data, and students are supposed to raise questions and, with their teachers' help, reach some conclusions. They use Flaherty's technique of visual suspense very effectively. For example, in part 1 of *Winter Sea-Ice Camp,* a man performs a mysterious operation, icing a hair onto a bone and laying it over a hole in the ice. Only slowly does the viewer realize that this will move when the seal comes for air, signaling the hunter to thrust his spear into the hole. Because of their pedagogical purpose, the Netsilik films focus on technology almost to the exclusion of social life, and there is no hint of Eskimo religious practices. The Netsilik had long since been Christianized, and perhaps they were unwilling or unable to re-enact their pagan practices.

In the end, this series came under attack from conservative activists and members of the U.S. Congress because of its espousal of cultural relativity. Schools quietly put the films in deep storage, and now they are hard to find.

AUSTRALIA

The longest tradition of ethnographic film exists in Australia, where Baldwin Spencer first shot Aboriginal dancers with a crude camera in 1904. Charles P. Mountford in the 1940s, Ian Dunlop and Roger Sandall in the 1960s, and, more recently, David and Judith MacDougall continued to record Aboriginal rituals and subsistence activities, but there has been little advance in the ethnographicness of the films. When anthropologists were involved, they were used as sound personnel and assistants, not researchers. Recently there has been a growing concern among Aboriginal men to preserve and protect the sanctity and secrecy of their own ceremonies. This has meant a virtual halt in the publication of descriptions and analyses of ceremonies in forms that might become available to Aboriginal women and uninitiated men. Now many films on rituals cannot be shown in Australia at all.

THE NATIVES' VIEW

When they offer interpretations of behavior, ethnographic films made by outsiders have generally been negligent in disentangling native from anthropological levels of interpretation. In ethnology, the distinction is essential. Two projects attempted to capture the native view on film, but they took very different approaches.

The Navajos Film Themselves

Sol Worth, a professor of communications, and John Adair, an anthropologist, with the assistance of Richard Chalfen, then a graduate student working with Worth, conducted an experiment in 1966 in which Navajo Indians made films about their own culture. The project was reported by Worth and Adair in 1972. A second edition of this book with an important new introduction and afterword by Chalfen, now a professor of anthropology, came out in 1997.

On the (Whorf-Sapir) assumption that the structure of language in some sense reflects or shapes the worldview of speakers of that language, and on the assumption that film, as a form of expression, is in some way analogous to language, Worth and Adair hypothesized that films made by Navajos would be in some fundamental sense Navajo.

Some twenty films were made by eight Navajos, and ten of these films are in distribution. None of the Navajos had used a movie camera before, and it is not clear how much of the results to attribute to inexperience and how much to "Navajo-ness." Most of the filmmakers had seen Hollywood films and television, and one was a self-professed admirer of French cinema, but one can only guess at the implications of these various influences.

And apparently no one fluent in Navajo had analyzed the data. Worth and Adair do make a convincing case for two major Navajo influences. First, most of the films have long sequences of someone walking. In *Navajo Silversmith,* fifteen minutes are spent on showing the silversmith walking in search of materials, and only five minutes on actually casting and finishing silver. This walking theme is very prominent in Navajo myths.

Also, the customary Navajo avoidance of direct eye contact is reflected in the general absence of full-face close-ups in the Navajo films. But, of course, to a non-Navajo these features would only be puzzling, or not even noticed, without Worth and Adair's analysis. Ethnography has traditionally involved translation, explanation, and analysis of one culture into the idiom of another. If Worth and Adair are right, then Navajo films would be somehow "in Navajo" and would therefore be the raw material for ethnography, not ethnography itself. The most valuable aspect of the project was to raise the question of the culturally specific nature of films. The implications of this are of great importance to ethnographic films. There is a great need for more research in this direction.

Japanese Tea

The Worth and Adair approach was to give Navajos film equipment but minimal instruction or direction, to encourage them to make films, and then to see if the resulting films contained anything that seemed specifically Navajo.

Donald Rundstrom and Ronald Rundstrom, with the help of Clinton Bergum, took a very different approach in *The Path*, a film of the Japanese tea ceremony. After long and intensive study of the tea ceremony and its philosophy, they designed the film not just to depict it but also to embody the aesthetic principles in its shots and sequences. They made a studied attempt to show the tea ceremony not only in the visual depiction but also in the very structure of the film. The Rundstroms were particularly concerned to show the yin-yang balancing of opposites and the management of energy, or the energy flow. The film is a mixture of ethnographic explanation and nearly inaccessible raw materials. It does show the progress of a tea ceremony as two women walk through a formal garden into a teahouse, where their hostess serves them tea. The occasional narrative gives words of explanation, instruction, or Zen obfuscation from famous tea masters. On the other hand, the filmmakers did not attempt to have the narration point out the subtler, deeper structural motifs. They have solved this problem by preparing an ethnographic companion for the film that describes in detail the history of the Japanese tea ceremony and the aesthetic principles of *d\o* (the way) and recounts the making of the film (Rundstrom, Rundstrom, and Bergum 1973).

More recently, there has been growing interest in filmmaking among peoples who previously were those filmed. See, for example, Chalfen 1997;

Turner 1991; Ruby 2000, 221–238; and especially a collection of articles in *Visual Anthropology Review* 11.2 (1995).

INSTITUTIONALIZATION OF ETHNOGRAPHIC FILM

During the decades since 1963, the year in which *Dead Birds* appeared, ethnographic film shared in the rich growth of the social sciences and became institutionalized, bureaucratized, and established.

There is now a section of the American Anthropological Association, the Society for Visual Anthropology, which regularly sponsors panels at the AAA annual meeting and also, for a day and a half just preceding the meeting, sponsors the Conference on Visual Anthropology organized by Thomas Blakely, at which works in progress are presented. The SVA awards annual prizes in several categories for ethnographic films and on occasion makes Lifetime Achievement Awards. The journal of the SVA, *Visual Anthropology Review,* appears semiannually and *American Anthropologist,* the journal of the AAA, has a visual anthropology section until recently under the editorship of Jeff D. Himpele. Ethnographic film has been the subject of degree programs at UCLA, the University of Southern California, Temple University, California State University at San Francisco, and the University of South Carolina.

Internationally there is comparable activity. The Granada Centre for Visual Anthropology at Manchester University, the Institute for Scientific Film (IWF) at Göttingen University, and the Musée de l'Homme in Paris are important centers, but there are countless other centers and programs, as well as annual, biennial, and occasional conferences around the world. For new generations of ethnographic filmmakers and viewers of ethnographic films, surely the best is yet to come.

THREE

THE ATTRIBUTES OF
ETHNOGRAPHIC FILM

In the first chapter, we discussed the general nature of film and of ethnography and what we can expect of the two together. The second chapter was a selective foray into the history of ethnographic film, focused on four filmmakers and designed to trace the development of various ideas that could make film more ethnographic. In this chapter, we shall analyze in greater detail the various attributes of film that affect its ethnographicness. This will be a critical examination and a guide to understanding ethnographic films of the past, and it will suggest standards for making ethnographic films in the future. It is an attempt to systematize what has emerged after years of ethnographic filmmaking. Of course, there are those for whom films are purely art, to be experienced and appreciated in darkened rooms, and there are filmmakers for whom making films is an intuitive, aesthetic, emotional act of creation. For them this book is bound to appear as the overintellectualization of an essentially experiential enterprise. But it is basic to ethnography, as well as the other social sciences, that we have a rational, explicit methodology. And thus films that attempt to achieve ethnographicness must share this quality of rational, explicit methodology.

The discussion in this chapter is ordered around several attributes that are common to all films, however ethnographic they may be. Most of these attributes are really continua. And films can be located somewhere along the line of variation. In some, there will be clear ethnographic choices for one value over another. For others, the choices will be a matter of personal inclination or ethnographic strategy and will only determine the sort of ethnography that the film presents. Taken together, the attributes allow one to make a profile description of a film. I still do not think that it is useful to try to define ethnographic film or to say whether a particular film is or is not ethnographic. But the use of the attribute profile will make quite explicit what is meant by ethnographicness in film and will allow us to appreciate—on the basis of a complex but explicit set of criteria—the relationship of a film to ethnography.

In the first edition of this book I was more inclined to use these attributes to judge films as being more or less ethnographic (but not to call some films non-ethnographic). With another thirty years of films to consider, it now seems clear that there are many ways to make films of ethnographic value.

This is an attempt to bring a nuanced appreciation of ethnographic film to the fore. We are conditioned by film reviews in the popular press to read a film title and immediately thereafter see the grade, be it four stars or several thumbs up or down. There are books claiming to rate, for example, "more than 18,000 movies!" In my classes I try to get students to begin with an analysis of a film, but many papers or discussions still start off with "I really liked this film" or "This was a really bad film." Of course, in real life, films live or die by such immediate reactions. But the problem is that once having committed oneself in that way, it is difficult to think out the qualities of film that we shall now explore.

This chapter is divided into three parts, each a more systemic treatment of the attributes than the preceding part. First we shall explore at some length the principles underlying each attribute. Then we shall make a succinct definition of each attribute and diagram that attribute as an attribute dimension with examples of specific films that illustrate the various points along this dimension. In the final part of the chapter, we shall examine the attributes as a grid on which a profile of ethnographicness can be drawn for any particular film.

THE ATTRIBUTES

Basic Technical Competence

One of the most unambiguous criteria for any film is simple technical cinematographic competence: the images should be focused and exposed so as to be visible; the sound, especially when it is in the language of the intended audience, should be clear enough to be audible; and the editing should be free of accidental mistakes and errors due to incompetence. Today, with most film shot on videotape, such factors are no longer of great analytical importance.

1. Appropriateness of Sound

Although one tends to think of film as a visual medium, in fact nearly all ethnographic films have a sound track, as do all films shot in video, and the relation of the aural to the visual is of great significance.

TABLE 3.1 APPROPRIATENESS OF SOUND

Inappropriate (e.g., orchestral music, heavy narration)	Moderate narration	Natural, synchronous sound
Nanook (1949)	Dead Birds Dani Sweet Potatoes Dani Houses	Post-1960s films

The appropriateness of sound may vary greatly from scene to scene within a film. The extreme in inappropriateness was reached in the 1949 version of *Nanook of the North*, which has both full orchestra and a wordy, redundant narration. Most films shot on film or video since the late 1960s use natural, synchronous sound.

When actual film was used, we had to distinguish synchronous sound from wild sound. Synchronous sound is the sound recorded at the same time as the film was shot, with camera and tape recorder working in precise synchrony. Wild sound is any other sound: it may be of the same sort of behavior or plausible background noises, postsynchronized to the image to give the illusion of true synchronous sound; it may be a read narration; it may be mood music; it may be a mixture of several of these. When a video camera is used for recording, synchronous sound is automatic. One would have to seriously disable a video camera to avoid sync sound.

When the sound includes speech in an exotic language, other problems arise that can be handled in various ways. Actually, much human use of language is so repetitive and so redundant with other sorts of behavior that speech can often be left untranslated and the audience loses very little information.

This point is especially well illustrated by *Nawi*, a film by David and Judith MacDougall about the Jie of Uganda. Through most of the film the people are simply sitting around, doing minor tasks, and talking a lot about very little. Bronislaw Malinowski coined the phrase "phatic communion" for this: "flow of language, purposeless expressions of preference or aversion, accounts of irrelevant happenings, comments on what is perfectly obvious . . . a type of speech in which ties of union are created by the mere exchange of words" (1923, 314–315). An occasional subtitle is enough to give us a sense of what is being said. *Nawi* was an early attempt to capture the ordinary low-energy action so characteristic of most people much of the time. Today it is much more common to hear such chatter, but, interestingly, audiences resent not having it all translated even when that would add little to the scenes.

An Argument about a Marriage and *The Feast,* both about high-energy events, use occasional subtitles in English so that the audience can follow the gist of an argument. In *The Nuer* and in *Rivers of Sand,* there are interview sequences in which, after someone makes a long statement in his own language, it is translated in the English narration. Direct dubbing of English, as is often done in commercial films, has not been tried with ethnographic films. None of these alternatives is totally satisfactory. One wants to savor the experience of seeing and hearing someone expressing herself in her own language, and one also wants to understand what is being said. But except for the obvious perils of mistranslation, there are no major problems of misleading distortion in synchronous sound.

The skillfully postsynchronized wild sound of pre-video films is quite a different matter. All the sound in *Dead Birds* is postsynchronized and covers a wide range. For the most part, Michael Rockefeller, Gardner's soundman, tried to record wild sound to cover each shot that Gardner made. Then, when Gardner came to edit his footage, he could use the most appropriate passages from Rockefeller's tapes. But when I filmed Dani house construction and horticulture two years later, I did not attempt to record sound. (At that time I was alone with the Dani and could not manage being soundman in addition to anthropologist and cameraman.) When I came to edit *Dani Sweet Potatoes* and *Dani Houses,* I decided not to go back to Rockefeller's tapes for appropriate wild sound because it simply wouldn't have been a close enough fit.

Music. To me, music is inevitably a distraction except when it is the sound of the events actually happening when the visuals were shot or, like the wild sound of the orchestra in *Trance and Dance in Bali,* when it is very appropriate to the visuals. The most common sort of music in ethnographic films is folk songs or instrumental music from the particular culture, but too often it appears in quite inappropriate contexts. It may seem somewhat harsh to criticize such music, because it is undeniably pleasant, audiences enjoy it, and it fills in those silences that cinema convention has declared to be abominable. But the main criterion for ethnographic films should not be the quantity of information and impressions and sensory enjoyment they can convey but rather the successful conveyance of information. The primary criterion for a sound track should be that it reinforces the visuals by providing very complementary information or that it at least is neutrally silent and does not work in opposition to the visuals by introducing vastly new information.

But I must acknowledge that recently my students disagree with this strong stand. Many of them are used to a constant musical background, even while studying, so any music on film is welcome and not distracting.

53

2. Narration

Narration consists of explanatory sentences read along with the visuals. It is almost impossible to have a narration that does not detract and distract from the visuals. Most ethnographic films show us totally exotic scenes: strange people wearing strange clothing doing strange things. Even if we focus our entire awareness on the scenes, we can barely take them in. But to have someone standing at our side telling us information in English as we are trying to watch the film must split our attention, and we lose much from both the auditory information and the visual scene. The purest solution to this problem was reached by the Netsilik Eskimo films, which have no narration at all, only postdubbed natural sound. These films treat simple subjects lengthily and redundantly, and they are meant to be shown by instructors who can answer questions and direct students' discussions. Actually, much is clarified by the progress of the events themselves. But most ethnographic films must cover more activities less redundantly and are somewhat more self-contained. So narrations are almost inevitable, in some form or another.

Narrations vary tremendously, but much of the important variation can be summarized in terms of two dimensions. One dimension can be called "added information" and concerns the amount of information that the narration adds to the film beyond what is contained in the visual images; the other dimension can be called "visual relevancy" and concerns the degree to which the narration is relevant to the visual images.

At one end of the continuum is the banal redundant sort of narration, so typical of the worst "documentary" film, which tells us things that are perfectly obvious from the visuals. We hear "and the rains fell" as we see rain falling. This sort of narration is closely related to the visual images but adds no information at all. A prime example of this style is found throughout the series of otherwise valuable films called the *People of the Australian Western Desert.* These films concentrate on technological processes, and most of the action is immediately understandable or is soon explained by the next actions. Nearly every word of the narration of all the films in this series is redundant with the visuals. At best, there are the proper nouns—names of people, of grasses, or of lizard species—which are really added information.

At the other extreme lies narration that is used to carry a story line when in fact the visuals show nothing of the sort. In some of the more exciting sections of *Dead Birds,* the excitement exists only in the narration, and the visuals are short, bland, scenic inserts. These sections are cinematically weak, but the narration is essential to carry the thread of the story while important events happened that could not possibly have been filmed. The amount of

TABLE 3.2 NARRATION

No narration or subtitles	Redundant, overly wordy, unrelated	Optimally demystifying and relevant to the visuals
Hanunoo	Nanook (1949)	Dani Sweet Potatoes
Netsilik Eskimo series	Dead Birds	Dani Houses
Forest of Bliss		Les maîtres fous
		The Lion Hunters
		Rivers of Sand

If narration is used at all, it is most effective when sparse and very closely related to the visuals, explaining or adding only minimal information needed to demystify behavior that cannot be explained visually. Redundant banal comments that add no new information (statements like "the rains fell") are often used simply to fill the air with words, as was the case with the 1949 sound version of *Nanook*. In films made in the late 1950s and early 1960s (like *Dead Birds*), before synchronous sound was possible, narrations tended to be wordy and attempted to convey masses of ethnographic information that had little basis in the visuals. In films by Jean Rouch, like *The Lion Hunters* and *Les maîtres fous*, narrations were used to explain and translate symbolic aspects of ceremonies that simply could not be elucidated in a purely visual manner. In *Rivers of Sand*, the sound track is mainly synchronous sound, with only a few explanatory lines of narration. After the 1960s, local voices began to take the place of outsiders' narrations.

added information is very high, because the words have hardly any relation to the visual images.

Within the optimal zone we can distinguish two styles of narration. In one, the words are used to explain or to clarify visual mysteries. In the other, the words put an act or event into the larger cultural context.

The two major misuses of narration, which fall outside the "optimal zone," are information redundancy and information overloading. The former is unnecessary; the latter could better be handled in printed form.

This scheme is fairly abstract. Applying its principle to criticism or to the making of a specific film involves a series of judgments that are often extremely difficult. For example, what is the line between necessary contextualization and overburdened esoterica?

Robert Flaherty, in his earlier, silent films, pushed the visual potential of film by creating and then resolving mysteries visually. The Netsilik Eskimo series does the same, using carefully chosen wild sound without narration. A close comparison between the Netsilik Eskimo films and the *Australian Western Desert* series is revealing. Both series were made in the mid-1960s, and both were about technological processes of a foraging group. The Netsilik budget was obviously much greater than the Australian budget, and the Netsilik films have excellent synchronized sound, whereas the Australian films lack even wild sound. If the Australian films omitted narration, they would be essentially silent films, and silent films seem to be anathema to many. But since the Australian narrations add so little, the films are, for all practical purposes, silent films. If one views any of them with the sound turned off—as I did once, by accident—it is clear how much more effective they are if the viewer can really engage in the visuals, without the distraction of the narration.

An interesting question comes to mind: If the narration is so redundant with the visuals, it may be meaningless, but is it really distracting? Or perhaps might it not assist viewers to concentrate on the visuals? I doubt it. In the Netsilik films, the viewer is left alone and has to work to understand. I would say that this understanding will be much more real than if one had information prechewed, as it were. This question could easily be studied in an experimental situation where the same film was used with and without redundant narration to two different groups and then each group was tested to see which had learned the most from the film. (Throughout this book, I am taking positions that could actually be tested. They seem reasonable, even obvious, but the next step is obviously to subject them to empirical testing.)

The Flaherty films, the Netsilik films, and the *Australian Western Desert* films all deal with technological processes, which are more amenable to a heavily visual clarification than are rituals. In films of rituals, where so much of the meaning is on the abstract, symbolic, verbal level, words are essential. In *Pomo Shaman,* the sparse commentary consists of statements by the shaman herself, recorded after the ceremony, as she describes what she is doing and how it felt to her. In Jean Rouch's films *Les maîtres fous* and *The Lion Hunters,* both dealing with complex ritual, a narrator gives what seems to be the native explanation of the different actions. Similarly, in *We Believe in Niño Fidencio,* the narration holds closely to the participants' explanation of the rituals. In *Anastenaria,* the narration gives a frankly ethnographic, or analytical, view of the ceremony.

Both the native understanding and the analytical, ethnographic understanding are essential ingredients of ethnographic presentation. But there are real advantages in using the native view in the film and saving the ethnographic analysis for a written report. When the native statement is coupled with the native behavior, they reinforce each other and increase the immediacy of the film experience. The analysis is essential, but it is a removed line of thought and has the effect of distancing the viewer from the film.

In *Dani Sweet Potatoes,* I tried to keep the narration down to an absolute minimum, using it only to explain actions that have been confusing or incomprehensible to an audience. And then, on Carroll Williams's advice, I laid each narration line in toward the end of a scene in order to engage the audience and give them time to be puzzled and, perhaps, to solve the mystery themselves.

One solution would be the use of only synchronous sound, without any narration. The use of the printed ethnographic companion to films would relieve the narration of much expository burden. Then much background information could be printed, rather than narrated, and ethnographic filmmakers could concentrate on making their films more filmic. But in practice it is difficult to make both film and print conveniently available to audiences. Another solution is the interactive DVD, which can in effect provide footnotes to films. Peter Biella has been experimenting with such materials, but they are still far from common.

3. Ethnographic Basis

Underlying all these considerations is a single one: an ethnographic film must be based on ethnographic understanding. The more successfully a film has this understanding, the more ethnographic it will be. However, this is no simpleminded recipe like "stir in heaping spoonfuls of ethnography." If that alone were sufficient, we could turn over all ethnographic filmmaking to ethnographers and be assured of successfully ethnographic films. But in fact a film may be made by an informed ethnographer and still be a failure ethnographically. In making an ethnographic film, ethnographic understanding is useless unless it is transmuted by filmic imagination. But despite these cautions, the single best predictor of ethnographicness in a film is the extent to which an ethnographer was involved in the filmmaking.

The basis for this has already been discussed at some length in chapter 1. In ethnographic writing, the understanding and conclusions emerge through the process of data gathering, analyzing, writing, and rewriting and are constantly being refined and even changed up to the moment of publication. But in filmmaking, on the other hand, the initial act of shooting footage produces fixed images and so precludes much of the rewriting possible in ethnography. The result is that whatever ethnographic understanding can be applied to the film must be present beforehand.

Perhaps the best model for ethnographic filmmaking is *The Feast* (see chapter 2). The filmmaking began only after the ethnography was completed, and the film itself was made by a filmmaker (Timothy Asch) working in

TABLE 3.3 ETHNOGRAPHIC BASIS

Uninformed by ethnography	Deeply shaped by ethnographic understanding
Grass	
	The Feast
Dead Birds	
Dani Sweet Potatoes	
Dani Houses	
	Neighborhood Tokyo
	I Love You

The degree to which an ethnographic film has been informed by ethnographic understanding is difficult to determine with real confidence, but one obvious indicator is the role (if any) that an ethnographer had in the filmmaking. Some films, like *Dead Birds* and *The Feast,* were made as part of an ethnographic study. At the other extreme is *Grass* (on the Bakhtiari of Persia), a remarkable film in its own way, made by keen observers but quite uninfluenced by ethnographic understanding.

the field in close collaboration with the ethnographer (Napoleon Chagnon). In this approach there is maximal opportunity for the fully digested ethnographic understanding to shape the film. Other films, such as *Dead Birds, Dani Sweet Potatoes,* and *Childhood Rivalry in Bali and New Guinea,* were shot by ethnographers as research was underway and thus had considerable ethnographic input.

4. Explicit Theory

In the not so distant past, much ethnography was fairly atheoretical and descriptive. It seemed important to record as much as possible before cultural variety in the world vanished. This was a sort of salvage ethnography. Today, despite globalization, cultures seem more robust, the interest in salvage ethnography has waned, and purely descriptive ethnography has yielded to more theoretically based studies.

Now ethnographic films also are more likely to be explicitly based on theory. Timothy Asch saw his Yanomamö film *The Feast* as a visual gloss on Marcel Mauss's classic study of exchange, *The Gift* (1925). Alan Lomax's films (*Dance and Human History, Palm Play, Step Style*) illustrate his choreometrics coding and theory. *India's Sacred Cow* is based on Marvin Harris's materialistic explanation of the Hindu prohibition on eating zebu cattle. Ron Simons's *Latah* explores the hyperstartle syndrome in Malaysia as an example of a biocultural model.

TABLE 3.4 EXPLICIT THEORY

Pure description	Implicit theory	Explicit theory
Dani Houses	Dead Birds	India's Sacred Cow
Dani Sweet Potatoes	The Feast	Dance and Human History
	Latah	

Although film seems most suited for straight descriptions of growing sweet potatoes, building houses, and the like, some films do, with the help of narration, present theoretical statements more or less explicitly.

In the 1960s, Douglas Oliver puzzled about how to incorporate thinking about and analysis of social organization in film. Peter Loizos did just that in *Life Chances,* about Greek Cypriots; John Marshall and Timothy Asch tried it in two Ju/'hoansi films, *A Joking Relationship* and *An Argument about a Marriage.* And there is Jean Rouch's *Lion Hunters,* an account of tension between cattle herders and marauding lions on the upper Niger, framed in terms of Claude Lévi-Strauss's symbolic dualism.

5. Relation to Printed Materials

No ethnographic film can stand by itself. An ethnographic film must be supplemented by written ethnographic materials. Or, put the other way around, an ethnography is a written work that may be supplemented by film. It is easy to conceive of ethnographies that are words without pictures. In fact, most of the best ethnographies either have no pictures at all (especially in the case of journal articles) or have a few irrelevant snapshots. But it is impossible to conceive of ethnographies made up of pictures without words. Of course, ethnographies can be complemented by pictures. And the use of film to describe some things that words cannot describe is one of the major challenges of ethnographic film and is discussed in chapter 4.

But the ethnographic enterprise demands a depth of description and of abstract generalization that cannot be handled in pictures alone. And while a few words can be spoken as narration, they are inadequate to convey much, and in any case are so overpowered by the visuals that they are barely understood.

So an important criterion of the ethnographicness of any ethnographic film is the extent to which it is backed up by written material. One major purpose of the catalog *Films for Anthropological Teaching* (K. Heider and Hermer 1995) has been to list the ethnographic materials relevant to the various films.

TABLE 3.5 RELATION TO PRINTED MATERIALS

No relevant printed materials	Vaguely relevant printed materials	Fairly well supported by printed materials	Fully integrated with printed materials
Grass	*The Nuer*	*Dani Sweet Potatoes*	*The Path*
Farm Song		*Dani Houses*	*Forest of Bliss*
			Jero Tapakan films
			The Goddess and the Computer
		Dead Birds	

The degree to which an ethnographic film is supported by written materials about the culture and about the circumstances of the filmmaking ranges widely. For *Grass,* there is some casual material on the filmmaking but no ethnography; for *The Nuer,* there is ethnographic material on the culture but from a different time and place; for *Dani Sweet Potatoes* and *Dani Houses,* there are published materials on the subject of the films by the filmmaker-ethnographer; and for *Dead Birds,* there is extensive ethnography and a study guide. The Balinese films on Jero Tapakan are also supported by an analytic and descriptive monograph (Connor, Asch, and Asch 1986). Some films, like *Neighborhood Tokyo* (see Bestor 1989), *India's Sacred Cow* (see Harris 1979), *Life Chances* (see Loizos 1975), and *The Goddess and the Computer* (see Lansing 1991) were actually made after the supporting ethnographies.

An example of this is *Dead Birds,* which was accompanied by considerable literature about the Dani, the culture described in the film, and especially by an "ethnographic companion" (K. Heider 1972a), a short pamphlet that specifically ties the film to the ethnographic literature (and is now out of print). More of such study guides are beginning to appear, and they will greatly increase the ethnographicness of the films they accompany. In addition to the ethnographic companion for *The Path* (Rundstrom, Rundstrom, and Bergum 1973), several study guides were produced on the Marshalls' Kalahari films (see Reichlin 1974a–g, L. Marshall and Biesele 1974, and Reichlin and Marshall 1974) and on the Yanomamö films. Connor, Asch, and Asch wrote a book on the first four Jero Tapakan films from Bali (1986), and Gardner and Östör's book, *Making "Forest of Bliss,"* is indispensable (2001).

6. Voice: Point of View

A film without a point of view is inconceivable. The process of selecting and excluding images that goes into making a film must be based on some concept. Even if we imagine a film that is somehow constructed according to a table of random numbers, that film would be based on an obvious point of view. Dada as an artistic movement may have rejected rules, but it certainly had a point of view.

The label "propaganda film" is often fixed on a film with a particularly obvious point of view, especially when the film's position is different from that of the critic. Rather than trying to define "propaganda film," let us shift to the more defensible and useful proposition that all films express some point of view. The points of view may vary greatly in substance, in the consciousness with which they are employed, and in the explicitness with which they are expressed, but they do exist and we can examine any ethnographic film in terms of them.

This seems quite obvious, yet a fair amount of critical blood is shed over the question of whether or not films are "objective." Probably there will always be filmmakers who claim that they are just reporting the facts, just as there are ethnographers who might claim the same position. The university where I studied anthropology has for its motto the single word "Truth" (in Latin, of course). But for both ethnographers and filmmakers a more comfortable guide word would be "Truths," in recognition that there are many different approaches to understanding. The famous Japanese film *Rashomon,* by Akira Kurosawa, is pertinent here. Set in medieval Japan, the investigation of a death and (perhaps) a rape turns up four versions of the same events. In ethnography, "the Rashomon effect" refers to the many factors that can affect an ethnographer's account of a culture (K. Heider 1988). In ethnography or in ethnographic film, it really comes down to this: selectivity is inevitable, and the author and the filmmaker should be aware of their points of view, because in the end they cannot avoid responsibility for them.

There are many points of view. Some films are made by special interests or at least subsidized by them, with the expectation that they present the group's point of view or at least show the product or the brand (product placement). Basil Wright and John Grierson made *Song of Ceylon* for the Ceylon Tea Propaganda Board; the film consists mainly of poetic images of Ceylon, with some scenes of tea growing and preparation. Flaherty had engaged in the same very subtle imagery; *Nanook* was sponsored by Revlon Frères, a fur company, and one scene shows Nanook and his family at the company's trading post, exchanging furs for goods. Flaherty's *Louisiana Story* was subsidized by Standard Oil, and it includes a shot of an oil well in the bayou. But it would be difficult to pinpoint ways in which these commercial interests shaped the point of view of the film.

No Longer Strangers, made by the Regions Beyond Missionary Union

TABLE 3.6 VOICE: POINT OF VIEW

From the ethnographer		Mix of local and	
Implicitly	Explicitly	ethnographic voices	The local people tell us
Nanook	Dani Houses	Farm Song	Makiko's New World
Hanunoo	Dead Birds	Fit Surroundings	How to Behave
Forest of Bliss	Dani Sweet Potatoes	The Nuer	Box of Treasures
	Forest of Bliss	A Kalahari Family	
	(with book)	Number Our Days	

Ethnographies and ethnographic films were in the beginning told in the voice of the ethnographer or the filmmaker, almost always an outsider's voice. Whether in silent films or through an omniscient narrator, we heard and saw the point of view of that outsider. The advent of sync sound and video not only allowed local voices to be included in films but also stimulated the movement toward presenting local points of view to shape films. Some films like *Farm Song* and *A Kalahari Family* even presented conflicting local points of view. Films like *Number Our Days* and *How to Behave* also presented local points of view.

about its conversion of the Western Dani to Christianity, is cinematographically rather crude but very effective. It was made to show to church groups in the United States in order to publicize the Dani mission work, to raise money, and to recruit missionaries. The point of view is explicitly that of evangelical Christianity. Traditional Western Dani rituals are described as a satanic mockery of Christianity. In other ways pre-Christian Western Dani culture is denigrated by such narration lines as "dancing girls perform their duties" and by the statement that the Dani had no tools, only stone axes. And while the narration describes the joys of the Western Dani when they became Christian, the visuals show masses of Christian Western Dani who are sullen, unsmiling, and not obviously joyful. *No Longer Strangers* makes an interesting counterpoint to *Dead Birds*. It was filmed near the Grand Valley, and the Western Dani of *No Longer Strangers* are closely related to the Grand Valley Dani of *Dead Birds* in language and culture. Although audiences often react strongly to the point of view of *No Longer Strangers*, they rarely even recognize the much more subtle point of view that Gardner has built into *Dead Birds*. In fact, Gardner takes the usual anthropological position of accepting a culture's practices on its own terms. So he discusses the Dani practice of cutting off girls' fingers as a funeral sacrifice and shows many mutilated hands; he shows and discusses war, battles, ambush, and killing without making a moral judgment. In my ethnographic writings about the

Dani, I do the same (1997a, 133–136). But we must recognize that this amoral observation is as much a point of view as is the missionaries' condemnation.

Even *Dani Houses* expresses a point of view. It shows, with some respect, Dani housebuilding at a time when the Indonesian government was attempting to induce the Dani to change their house style on the grounds that traditional Dani houses were smoky and unsanitary.

In addition to commercial, political, religious, and philosophical points of view, we must consider the scientific point of view, or the ethnographic interpretation. Just as ethnographic writings usually choose one sort of interpretation out of many possible ones, so do ethnographic films. However, films are more likely than writings to stay close to a straight descriptive level. Films like *Dani Sweet Potatoes* and *Dani Houses* do not undertake any real theoretical interpretation of Dani horticulture or construction. *India's Sacred Cow* is an explicitly polemical film. Different narrators argue different interpretations of the issue, although the film clearly favors Marvin Harris's cultural materialistic point of view. Some films use the native interpretation of events. For example, *Appeals to Santiago* used a first-person narration to describe the cargo ritual of the Chiapas Mayan and to present the explicit Mayan rationale that the ceremony is to honor the saints and has no economic function.

In the ethnographic tradition, the native explanation is an important datum, one which may agree with an ethnographic interpretation or which may be opposed to an ethnographic explanation. In *Appeals to Santiago,* the Mayas explain the Chiapas cargo ritual as an expression of Christian piety and deny that it is a competitive prestige-seeking institution. Frank Cancian (1965) has analyzed the same institution from an economic standpoint, showing how it functions to even out wealth in exchange for prestige stratification. Neither the Mayans nor Cancian are wrong, but from one we hear the explicit or manifest function, and from the other an implicit, latent function. (And this hardly exhausts the possibilities, for other analysts could make other analyses.)

For example, in *Les maîtres fous,* Jean Rouch explains the Hauka ceremony in psychological terms as a cathartic experience that releases hostility toward the colonial government and then allows the natives to return to their submissive daily occupations. In *The Turtle People,* Brian Weiss explains Miskito Indian subsistence in ecological terms and argues that the Miskito are destroying the turtle population for short-term financial rewards but will experience eventual economic disaster when the turtle boom is over. In *The Feast,* Asch analyzes a Yanomamö intervillage feast in terms of Marcel Mauss's gift exchange (Mauss 1925). The Rundstroms and Bergum show the

Japanese tea ceremony in *The Path* in terms of its symbolic structure, and Susannah Hoffman in *Kypseli* analyzes the Greek village in terms of sexual division of labor.

Each of these films utilizes only one of several possible theoretical points of view to analyze a situation. But this is a legitimate ethnographic strategy, and the films cannot be faulted for not including all possible points of view. A legitimate criticism might be that they misused a type of explanation or that they chose an inappropriate type of explanation. But in any case, they are more ethnographic than a film like *Dani Sweet Potatoes,* in the sense that they attempt to move beyond ethnographic description to ethnographic explanation. This is also a more hazardous course, for it is much easier to make a satisfactory descriptive film than to achieve a film whose description *and* explanation are above attack.

7. Holism: Behavioral Contextualization

Although the holistic approach to human behavior is one of the hallmarks of anthropology, holism is not so much a theory as it is an attitude that characterizes anthropological research and distinguishes it from other sorts of social science research. Holism is reflected in the typical ethnographic research strategy of living in the midst of a society and making extensive observations of many events; and it is reflected in the typical ethnographic account, where the emphasis is on the interrelationships of many facets of a culture or a society. Ethnography places great emphasis on the context of behavior. Ethnography is extensive, in comparison with the more intensive interests so typical of sociological or psychological research.

The anthropological emphasis on holism accords very well with the capability of film to show things and events in physical and temporal context. But just as the mere fact of living in a culture does not guarantee holistic ethnography, so merely shooting film does not assure holistic ethnographic film. Some basic anthropological principles, or corollaries of the principle of holism, are directly pertinent to the problems of ethnographic film. They have to do with contextualization of behavior and what we can call whole people, whole bodies, and whole acts, to be discussed below.

Contextualization is a basic but easily misunderstood concept or imperative. At one extreme it is obvious: things or events must not be treated in isolation; they have meaning only in context. On the other hand, it is clearly impossible to describe everything about everything. But it seems safe to say that although no film (or ethnography) has been hurt by overcontextualiza-

TABLE 3.7 HOLISM: BEHAVIORAL CONTEXTUALIZATION

Isolated, decontextualized		*Well contextualized*
Wooden Box	*Dani Houses*	*Dead Birds*
A Joking Relationship	*Dani Sweet Potatoes*	*The Goddess and the Computer*
		I Love You
		Box of Treasures

Contextualization is a measure of the degree to which a film sets behavior in its cultural and physical context. Of course, no film can make a complete contextual statement. And in some senses a short single-concept film may be contextualized not by itself but by other similar films (as the several short Ju/'hoansi films are) or by written materials (as with the two shorter Dani films). J. Stephen Lansing's *The Goddess and the Computer* is explicitly holistic in linking Balinese religious activity to the rice irrigation system. *Box of Treasures* sets Kwa Kwaka' Wakw art into its cultural and historical setting.

tion, many are flawed by inadequate contextualization. The precise degree of contextualization that should be achieved in an ethnography or a film is, in the end, a matter of judgment.

One can speak of contextualization in terms of cultural aspects. For example, I have often heard *Dead Birds* criticized for its lack of attention to Dani women. This is really the common but veiled complaint that the critic wanted a different film. While *Dead Birds* focuses on Dani men's life, it actually does show many aspects of women's life in the gardens, at the brine pool to get salt, and at ceremonies. But the film is about Dani men, and in Dani society the women are peripheral to the political, ritual, and warfare activities that concern the men. (I have speculated [2004] about the shape of the film if we had been the Radcliffe Peabody Expedition, made up of women, instead of the Harvard Peabody Expedition, and the films and books had been produced by female anthropologists and filmmakers.)

In other respects, *The Nuer* shows many acts taken out of context, presumably for aesthetic but not ethnographic reasons. *Grass* is another classic case of decontextualization, for although we see at great length the dramatic march of the Bakhtiari herdsmen over the mountains of Persia to their summer pastures, we learn practically nothing of the social, political, or economic context of this movement. The march exists as a brilliant, isolated act.

Mokil, which deals with overpopulation on a Micronesian atoll, and *Rivers of Sand,* about sex roles in an Ethiopian tribal society, are particularly notable attempts to handle the complexities of these topics through film.

Taking overpopulation or sex roles as the central fact, each film explores the ramifications and implications of that fact in a meandering, often repetitive, but quite contextualized fashion.

At the other extreme is the short film that deals intensively but not contextually with a single narrow subject. An excellent example of this is the thirty-three-minute film on the Kwa Kwaka' Wakw (Kwakiutl) with the strange title *Wooden Box: Made by Steaming and Bending.* The film shows a master craftsman making a wooden box. It is a fascinating tour de force, but without other knowledge of Kwa Kwaka' Wakw woodworking and symbolism, the viewer has no way of understanding the context of that act.

Three films about family dynamics—*Dadi's Family* (India), *Farm Song* (Japan), and *I Love You: Hope for the Year 2000* (Sumatra)—each set family tensions into wider behavioral contexts.

8. Physical Contextualization

In *Dead Birds,* Gardner used early shots very skillfully to establish the context of the landscape in which the action will take place. He used several long shots taken from a hill. First, in a long pan following a hawk that glides across the landscape, actually below the camera level, the bird is in focus and the landscape out of focus. But the narration at this point is dense and important, so the audience is allowed only an impression of the landscape. This shot is followed by another, also from the hilltop, that begins looking down into Weyak's village, then pans along a path to the gardens, then zooms out to a wide-angle view of gardens, no-man's-land, enemy country, and the far mountains. A later shot from the same high vantage point also begins at

TABLE 3.8 PHYSICAL CONTEXTUALIZATION

Little or no physical contextualization		Well set in the physical environment	
The Nuer	Jero Tapakan films	*I Love You*	*Fit Surroundings*
		The Goddess and the Computer	*Dead Birds*

It helps to have hills or tall buildings as vantage points from which to film the entire behavioral setting of the event, as in *Dead Birds, Neighborhood Tokyo,* or *Hanunoo. The Goddess and the Computer* uses maps and diagrams to help describe the field of action. But often the subject is so domestic (*Dadi's Family* or *Latah*) that there is little need for this contextualization.

Weyak's village and follows another trail out to Weyak's watchtower. Thus economically and dramatically and very visually, we are put into the Dani physical world (see K. Heider 2005).

The Nuer, in contrast, lacks such landscape contextualizing. Of course, in the flat Nuer country the filmmakers had no handy hilltop. And they may have felt that to use shots made from airplanes or helicopters would have been obvious and intrusive and would have destroyed the delicate ambience of their film. But ethnographically the necessity for this sort of contextualization—for example, showing a complete Nuer village, showing the cornfields, or showing the relationship of village to fields to pasture to river—could have overridden other considerations.

9. Reflexivity: The Ethnographer's Presence

The very presence of outsiders, be they ethnographers carrying out their research or filmmakers making films, inevitably has a myriad of influences on the subjects' behavior. Reflexivity implies both the acknowledgement of that presence and, more important, analyses of the effects of that presence. Most ethnographic filmmakers deny this effect and simply edit out any footage that reveals camera consciousness or too-blatant mugging. Admittedly, this is comparable to the general practice in ethnography, but it is one instance where the ethnographic practices can be followed too closely. The alternative is to build the outsider's presence into the structure of the film, to give some idea of how the people may be reacting to the outsiders, how questions are asked and answered, and the nature of deliberate intrusions, experiments, or the like that the outsiders are making.

Some ethnographic films do make the anthropologist the major focus of the film. *Margaret Mead's New Guinea Journal* follows Mead in her return visit to Manus, forty years after her original fieldwork there. *Gurkha Country,* made by John and Patricia Hitchcock in Nepal, shows the Hitchcocks themselves living and doing research among the Gurkha. And *A Man Called "Bee": Studying the Yanomamö* presents anthropologist Napoleon Chagnon at work in the Venezuelan jungles. *Neighborhood Tokyo* follows Theodore Bestor around the area that he studied, and Alison and Marek Jablonko show Maurice Godelier investigating *The Baruya Story.* Barbara Myerhoff is very much a presence in *Number Our Days,* as is David Plath in *Fit Surroundings.*

In fact, considering that the major use of ethnographic film is in introductory anthropology courses, it is surprising that there have not been more filmic attempts to show how anthropologists actually work. The success

TABLE 3.9 REFLEXIVITY: THE ETHNOGRAPHER'S PRESENCE

Ethnographer's presence ignored by film	Ethnographer's presence mentioned	Ethnographer shown interacting and gathering data
Dead Birds	The Moontrap	Fit Surroundings
Dani Houses		Chronicle of a Summer
Dani Sweet Potatoes		Neighborhood Tokyo
		Number Our Days
		I Love You

By judiciously incorporating the ethnographer and the filmmaker into the film, and analyzing their effect on the behavior being recorded, a film can become more self-conscious about the sorts of information it communicates. Jean Rouch was the leading practitioner of this approach. His *Chronicle of a Summer,* which is not simply about Paris in 1960 but more about how an anthropologist and a sociologist go about investigating Paris in 1960, illustrates the strengths of using the ethnographic presence. *Dead Birds* and the two short Dani films, on the other hand, omit the presence of the ethnographers completely. In the middle ground is *The Moontrap;* although we never see the filmmakers, we are told that the revival of whale trapping, which is the subject of the film, was done at their instigation. Likewise, in *I Love You: Hope for the Year 2000,* we never actually see either ethnographer or filmmaker, but they are integral and explicit actors in the events described.

of written accounts of fieldwork like Claude Lévi-Strauss's *Tristes tropiques* (1955), Kenneth Read's *The High Valley* (1965), and many others suggests that comparable films would be most welcome.

The most ambitious film in this vein was one of the first, *Chronicle of a Summer* (1961), made by anthropologist Jean Rouch and sociologist Edgar Morin to capture the mood of Paris in the summer of 1960. Throughout the film, the two men are very visible and present. The film opens with Morin interviewing a young woman and directing her to do street interviews, to ask people, "Are you happy?" Morin and Rouch have several more talks with people, probing their psyches. Then, at a group discussion, Rouch announces that the film should turn to consider politics—Algeria and the Congo. More discussions with students, workers, and artists are followed by a sequence in a screening room where Rouch, Morin, and the subjects, who have just seen the film, discuss it, themselves, and each other. And finally, Rouch and Morin alone in the Musée de l'Homme, strolling past the relics of other cultures safely enclosed in glass, discuss whether they have shown the reality of their own culture in the film. *Chronicle of a Summer* is a richly provocative film in the extent to which it reveals and attempts to analyze the methodological mystery of ethnography, but as yet no other ethnographic films have risen to its challenge.

Nevertheless, ethnographic films have acknowledged and used the presence of the outsiders in various other ways. In Adrian A. Gerbrands's *Matjemosh,* the narrator, supposedly speaking the thoughts of the Asmat (West New Guinea) wood-carver, tells of his wife's shyness before his friend Gerbrands and of his own amusement when Gerbrands asks him to make drawings of Asmat designs with a felt-tip pen on paper for the film. (Unfortunately, since Matjemosh speaks in a Dutch-British accent, the effect is somewhat lost.)

In *An Argument about a Marriage,* one of John Marshall's short Kalahari films, we are told that the conflict was precipitated when the Marshall expedition freed and brought back some Bushmen from enforced labor on a farm. And midway through the argument, when one man attempts to invoke the Marshalls on his side, the other replies, according to the subtitle, "Screw the Marshalls." And in *Death by Myth,* the fifth part of Marshall's *Kalahari Family,* we see a great deal of Marshall himself, involved in bitter arguments about the fate of the Ju/'hoansi.

In *The Nuer,* an old man makes statements that seem to be responses to questions, although we never see or hear the questioner. *I Love You: Hope for the Year 2000* was made by filmmaker Kathrin Oester and anthropologist Heinzpeter Znoj. We never see either of them, but the narrator is a woman, supposedly the anthropologist, and at times we hear the man's voice asking a question. The film works well in showing some of the problems of fieldwork, but one has to ignore the reversal of roles.

But there are many styles of ethnographic film, and some are better suited than others to including anthropologists in the film. It is always possible to explain the film crew's presence in written material that can be used to supplement the film, as, for example, the Rundstroms did in their essay (1973) on making *The Path.*

On the whole, the reasons in favor of showing the ethnographic presence in an ethnographic film seem to me to be compelling. In the first place, the ethnographic presence is, after all, part of the behavior being filmed, and so by including some of this in the film, we can see that part of the behavior and form some idea of how it affected the rest. In the second place, since the outsiders are mediating the information about one culture to an audience from another culture, including them in the film personalizes the mediation and, by making it more understandable, makes it more effective. The impersonal distancing effect of omitting the ethnographer decreases the ease with which an audience can understand a film; it also carries a political implication of noninvolvement, of treating the people as impersonal objects. This is a subtle matter, which I have thought about in regard to my own research. When I do research among the Dani, they are, inescapably, the subjects of my study but, I hope, not merely the objects I study and describe. Even when I quantify and generalize, I try not to lose sight of the fact that they are people who matter. Now, there are certainly ways to communicate this in films without showing the ethnographer, but the ethnographic presence is one way of adding this effect. (Of course, in making *Dani Sweet Potatoes* and *Dani Houses,* when I was both ethnographer and entire film crew, it would have been exceedingly difficult to have included myself or the effect of my presence in the films.) When we were filming *Dead Birds,* Robert Gardner had considered including shots of the Harvard Peabody Expedition members. But that was in 1961, and at that time it didn't seem appropriate or necessary (although Jean Rouch, making *Chronicle of a Summer* at the same moment, did try it).

There certainly can be drawbacks to the ethnographic presence in a film if, for example, shots of the ethnographer are included without concern for their relation to the action in the film. Obviously the idea is not merely to prove that an ethnographer and filmmaker were present, and to give them a chance to be movie stars, but rather to show the manner in which their presence was felt. There is sometimes a thin line between the good and bad uses of the ethnographic presence.

10. Whole Acts

Cinema is ideally suited to present process, or behavior through time. But in order to show the structure of a whole act, especially in nonstaged shooting of naturally occurring behavior, one must know how to anticipate an action. Acts can be said to have beginnings, peaks, and endings. The unknowledgeable observer or filmmaker will notice an act as it is climaxing but will not have enough experience to know that it will happen soon enough to pick up the beginning and will not have enough sense of the act to follow it past its end. An especially telling film is Hugo van Lawick's *Baboons of Gombe.* Van Lawick had been filming primates, especially chimpanzees, at Gombe Stream Reserve in Tanzania for a decade. With his experience, van Lawick was able to follow a variety of acts, large and small, almost from before their beginnings, through their peaks to their endings.

The criterion that whole acts are desirable refers to the selective use of structural features of the act. It is not possible to demand that everything

TABLE 3.10 WHOLE ACTS

Fragmentary bits of acts		*Beginnings, peaks, and ends of acts*
Primate	Dani Houses	Forest of Bliss
The Nuer	Dani Sweet Potatoes	The Cows of Dolo Ken Paye
	Dead Birds	The Hunters

Ongoing, naturally occurring behavior can be analyzed and understood as a series of acts, of greater or lesser magnitude, many occurring simultaneously but often not coterminously; and each of the acts has a beginning, a peak, and an end, not to mention prehistories (antecedents) and consequences (outcomes). Some ethnographic films, like *The Cows of Dolo Ken Paye* and *The Hunters,* are particularly successful in portraying whole acts in this sense of the concept, while films like *The Nuer* and *Primate* are made of fragments of behavior.

An act can be of any length, measured in seconds, hours, days, or years. Acts are usually presented in their actual sequences, but sometimes a film like *Forest of Bliss* presents the ritual process of death in separate scenes out of the real order, with the intent that the viewers will slowly put the actual sequence of events together in their minds.

about an entire act be shown. That is unrealistic realism. Two ethnographic films have attempted to approach this by having film time equal real time. But even in these films much had to be omitted. In Carroll Williams's *An Ixil Calendrical Divination,* the camera holds in close to the hands of the diviner as he lays out his pieces on a surface. Consequently, we do not see the interaction between the diviner and his patients, an interaction that surely gives the sensitive diviner as much information about the problem as the way in which his pieces fall on the board. In *The Path,* the Japanese tea ceremony is shown in real time, but in order to film it, the action was stopped and repeated many times, and so a part of the interaction between hostess and guests was lost to the film. It is conceivable that a short and simple act could be filmed by several cameras simultaneously and then projected on multiple screens. This would be an interesting exercise. But it would merely be the reproduction of reality, not the understanding and analysis of reality that are the basis of ethnology (or any other science).

Selection of shots is inevitable in filmmaking. The criterion of whole acts demands that the selection be done so as to present the important features of an act. Just as there are many different legitimate ethnographic approaches, so the selection may bring out different aspects of an act. It is not good to be dogmatic at this point. The Rundstroms selected shots in *The Path* to show yin-yang balance and energy management (Rundstrom, Rundstrom, and Bergum 1973). Other anthropologists might make quite different selections from the same event.

The whole act must be adequately represented by selective elements. And in this context, where we are speaking of the ethnographicness of film, we can say without hesitation that the selection should be done on the basis of some ethnographic understanding, and the adequacy of the whole act can be judged ethnographically.

What is a "whole act"? This is an extremely flexible concept, but useful nevertheless. Acts may last seconds; they may last years. There are acts within acts. And in the end the filmmaker or the ethnologist chooses which of the countless possible acts will be attended to. Harold Conklin's *Hanunoo* is an extreme example of incomplete acts. It is eighteen minutes of short clips. There is no attempt to follow through on any one act. (Yet it can serve as a study piece for getting an overall visual idea of Hanunoo life—see K. Heider 2004a). In *Dani Sweet Potatoes* and *Dani Houses,* I deliberately planned to show each step of the sweet potato cycle and of construction. But both films were narrowly conceived. I did not follow through and show how Dani houses were lived in, or much at all of how sweet potatoes were distributed and eaten. My whole focus at the time was on production, not distribution or consumption. If I were to remake these films today, they would be very different.

In *Dead Birds,* Gardner follows the entire salt-making process and all the major steps of a funeral (as well as we understood them in July 1961). In contrast, the initiation sequence in *The Nuer* is a sadly incomplete document. It shows a few peak moments, dwelling at length on the bloody forehead incisions. The film captures the most obvious events, but what it omits (presumably because they hadn't been filmed) are many important symbolic events that we know of from the ethnographic literature; and, presumably, from ignorance of the meaning of initiation itself, the film doesn't even follow the individuals into manhood.

Although Frederick Wiseman spent one month shooting and two hours of screen time on bits of scientific experimentation at the Yerkes Primate Research Center in Atlanta for his 1974 television film, *Primate,* the film never followed a single experiment as a whole act. This approach had interestingly different effects on different viewers. Laymen (including television critics) were simply horrified by the picture of senseless butchery in the guise of science; one friend of mine who is familiar with that sort of research could fill in the gaps for himself and was fascinated by the film; more thoughtful viewers reacted strongly against the film itself on the grounds that it made no attempt to communicate an understanding of primate research by presenting whole acts but only used scenes of gore to play on the audience's emotions and turn them away from such research.

BEGINNINGS

We can consider the wholeness of any act in terms of its beginning, its peak, and its ending. The beginnings are the most difficult to film because this really demands enough knowledge of the behavior to anticipate an act before it begins. In some acts, such as trance states, the transition from the previous, or "normal," stage into the altered state is of obvious importance. Trance is an extreme example, but it serves as a good model. When we speak of "an act," we mean some relatively definable behavioral event that is different from what preceded it and from what follows. If one is writing ethnography, it is easy to construct sentences after the fact that will describe the beginnings of an act. But it is much more difficult to have a camera at the right time and the right place to capture an act as it is beginning.

One ethnographic film that does this particularly well is *The Cows of Dolo Ken Paye,* made in a Kpelle village in Liberia by Marvin Silverman and James L. Gibbs Jr. The major act in the film is the resolution of a conflict over a cow that had been found in a farmer's field, was wounded by a machete blow, and died. The peak action began with the discovery of the wounded cow, and following the case from that moment was relatively easy. But thanks to Gibbs's intimate ethnographic understanding of the culture, the film was able to re-create the beginning of the act. It described the complex implications of rich men's cattle and poor men's farms; it incorporated still photographs that Gibbs had taken of a similar conflict years earlier and that had served as a precedent, and it even was able to include serendipitous footage of the culprit chopping a log with his machete, taken before the act. Thus, with the combination of luck and deep ethnographic understanding, the film was able to anticipate an act. The beginning of the act was approximated in the editing room, in a manner similar to the ex post facto written description of an ethnography. It may well be that this sort of reconstructed beginning is all that we can expect for many larger acts shown in ethnographic films.

PEAKS

Peak activity is the part of the act that involves the most energy and activity and draws the most attention. It is this peak activity that even the most uninformed filmmakers can capture. But there is a great danger of infatuation with peaks. Just because peaks are so obvious to see and easy to film, attention is distracted from other activity that may be less energetic but, in cultural terms, more important. John Heider (1974) discussed this in human potential encounter therapy, where a peak, or "blowout," is customarily followed by a long plateau of creative ecstasy. He describes how, in the early days of Esalen Institute, group leaders were preoccupied with achieving the peak experiences. Only gradually did they come to understand the importance of the postcathartic plateau. In ethnographic film, a similar preoccupation with peak drama can make for an exciting but superficial picture of an event. But I feel diffident about accusing specific films of this failing, since the full ethnographic facts are usually not available.

CLOSURE

The final part of the demand that ethnographic films show whole acts is the demand that they achieve some degree of closure: that acts or events are brought to some sort of completion.

We are familiar with the conventional symbols of closure that American cinema adopted from storytelling: the boy and the girl live happily ever after. A more cinematographic symbol of closure is the final shot of a sunset, preferably over an ocean. The power of the symbol is that we accept it as closure and feel satisfied. This is a kind of emotional satisfaction, different from the intellectual need for complete information.

In *The Nuer,* we are often brought into an important event, and before we learn its outcome, the subject is changed. In *Dead Birds,* on the other hand, Gardner's final philosophical statement about the Dani and death is a very personal attempt to give emotional closure to the entire film, probably for Gardner himself as well as for the audience.

Many ethnographic films do impose a punch-line structure. This is the structure of the joke that closes with a climactic punch line. But in fact, most behavior does not follow this pattern. It may reach a peak, or climax, but then slowly fades out into another act. Two of John Marshall's Kalahari films have particularly fine treatments of closure. In *The Hunters,* after the giraffe has been killed, we follow the bringing home of the meat, the distribution, and the eating. Then it is all recapitulation as one of The Hunters tells the story of the hunt, and when that is over, people slowly get up and disperse. In *Bitter Melons,* the final sequence shows men doing a dramatic ostrich courting dance. The final shot seems to hold forever as the men drop the dance, lie down to nap, or drift away. Still the shot holds, as two boys make a halfhearted attempt to revive the dance. Then they, too, become still. And finally, after all activity has slowed down to a stop, the shot is over. To hold a shot so long takes courage in shooting and courage in editing (it was edited by Frank Galvin). But *Bitter Melons* achieves an exceptional degree of closure through it.

DENSITY OF INFORMATION

The criterion of whole acts is one way of judging whether or not a film presents an adequate amount of information. From that perspective, a film that adequately shows an entire act has an adequate amount of information. The whole-acts criterion is a structural criterion, since it assumes that we can talk about a basic and necessary structure to behavior, the elements of which must be shown in film.

But we need another criterion that specifies the pure load of information presented in a film. It is quite possible for a film not only to show structurally excellent whole acts but also to have too much information. This is a danger to which ethnography is not subject. An article or a book can be made longer and can be broken up with chapters and subchapters. No one is forced to read an ethnography book straight through at a steady pace in one sitting. In fact, tables of contents and indexes are invitations to dip selectively. But films are designed to be seen without interruption from the beginning through to the end. Few people have the inclinations, the equipment, or the opportunity to use films like books. A couple of attempts were the shot-by-shot analysis section of the Ethnographic Companions to Films modules (e.g., K. Heider 1972a), and the monograph on the Balinese Jero films (Connor, Asch, and Asch 1986), which in effect translated the films shot by shot into the printed word and thus made the films available for convenient re-viewing.

The old joke about the book that told the little boy more than he wanted to know about penguins takes on a different meaning here. The boy could easily escape by not reading parts of the book. But if he had seen a film that presented more about penguins than he could understand, he would have a valid complaint.

One way in which a film can have too much information is a sort of non-ethnographic paradox, as in the initiation sequence of *The Nuer*. Not enough of the initiation is presented to make it understandable. Yet in another sense there is too much of the inadequate information. By this I mean that the film has created visual mysteries that go unexplained in either the visual or the aural channels of the film.

One might also argue that any film contains too much information. For someone whose research on microbehavioral data demands countless intensive viewings of a few frames of film, even twenty minutes of film, seen once at twenty-four frames each second, would be a painfully intolerable overdose of information, no matter how ethnographic the film. But the data of microbehavioral analysis must be distinguished from the grosser sorts of information that ethnographic films are designed to communicate. So it is legitimate to say that a film may have too little, too much, or appropriate amounts of information, depending on the audience.

This overloading of information is especially common in ethnographic films made by anthropologists. It seems reasonable to blame this on the anthropologists' familiarity with print where, as we have seen, more information can always be added in another (often unread) chapter or appendix, in such a way that it does not compromise the entire work. Most of the criteria discussed in this chapter are ethnographic criteria; the danger of information overload is one that cinematographers are much more sensitive to than are most anthropologists. The problem is to judge how much information is enough and to stop there.

The most usual and obvious locus of superfluous information is, of course, in the narration. I now think that I did this in *Dani Sweet Potatoes*. Since I had no sound other than the narration, I was self-conscious about having too much silence. Also, after showing a work print of the film to many different sorts of audiences, I was very aware of the sorts of questions that were usually asked, and I tried to use the narration to head them off. So, for example, over a shot of a large newly planted sweet potato bed, I described the other sorts of gardens and cultigens of the Dani. Now in fact, that information is available in print, and the view of the garden in itself, without narration, contains enough information to engage an audience. So here and elsewhere in *Dani Sweet Potatoes* the narration provides an overload of information.

Information overload can result from a narration that says too much, visuals that show too much, or a combination of narration and visual excesses. But this is a particularly difficult judgment to make. Much depends on the nature of the audience and the intensity with which the film is viewed. If an ethnographic film is shown on prime-time television to a mass audience, it can tolerate far less information than if it is only to be studied by advanced college classes in anthropology, who may see it more than once.

11. Narrative Stories

Flaherty is always considered a master storyteller, and some of his films reflect this. Although there is no real narrative story running through *Nanook*, he does realize a story in *Moana*, where the Samoan youth achieves manhood and wins his girl by undergoing the tattoo initiation ritual. In *The Hunters*, John Marshall tells a story of how the Ju/'hoansi shoot and track a wounded

TABLE 3.II NARRATIVE STORIES

Vignettes	Episodes loosely strung together	Complete story
Hanunoo	Latah	Timing Death
Song of Ceylon	Dani Sweet Potatoes	The Cows of Dolo Ken Paye
Nanook	Dani Houses	I Love You
	!Nai	Jaguar

Nanook follows an Inuit family and includes several whole acts, but it does not tell a complete story. *I Love You: Hope for the Year 2000,* on the other hand, has no whole acts but is built around the story of how marriages, which take place only once a year, are arranged in a central Sumatran village. We meet the young people who have hopes of being married, but they—and the anthropologist—are kept in suspense until the end of the film, the wedding day. James L. Gibbs Jr.'s *Cows of Dolo Ken Paye* is even more of a mystery story: in a Liberian village a calf is killed, and we watch the Kpelle legal system as it discovers and punishes the culprit.

giraffe for days in order to kill it and bring back meat for the camp. In *Dead Birds,* Gardner is able to create a story by following the events of war for the five months he was in the Grand Valley, as Weyak's group lose a boy to the enemy but finally restore a balance by killing one of the enemy.

Some films, like the Netsilik Eskimo series or *Dani Sweet Potatoes,* achieve a continuity not through the adventures of an individual but by following a technical process to completion. The weakest attempt at a story line, but one that ethnographic filmmakers sometimes try, is "a day in the life of the village." James L. Gibbs Jr. and Marvin Silverman's film of the Kpelle of Liberia, *The Cows of Dolo Ken Paye,* started out in this way, but partway through the filming they stumbled onto a dramatic legal case that became the subject of a quite different and much more focused film.

Bateson and Mead achieved another sort of continuity in their Balinese films by filming a few individuals, especially infants, over a long period to show the developmental process. *Karba's First Years* is a unique ethnographic film that traces the development of a Balinese boy through the major stages of early childhood. Few anthropologists studying child development have designed their research to follow individual characters as they grow up, but John Marshall's *!Nai,* edited from footage that Marshall shot over the years, does follow !Nai from childhood into adulthood.

Many ethnographic films are little more than series of vignettes, or "impressions." *The Nuer* is this sort of film: brilliantly filmed impressions of a cattle camp. An occasional event happens to occur: a marriage dispute, a mass healing ritual, an initiation, and an exorcism. But the filmmakers were not familiar enough with the culture to know what should be filmed in order to show complete and understandable event sequences. The prototype of the impressionistic vignette film is *Song of Ceylon,* made by John Grierson and Basil Wright for the Ceylon Tea Propaganda Board in 1934. It is a series of scenes, loosely organized into thematic sections.

A film may be thought of as having various levels of possibilities for continuity. The entire film may have a single theme, like *Dani Sweet Potatoes,* which follows the Dani horticulture sequence from clearing land, planting, weeding, and harvesting to cooking and eating. Practically every shot in the film contributes to that complex.

On a less inclusive level, a film may contain one or more shorter activity sequences. Edited throughout *Dead Birds* is a complete sequence of women producing salt, and another of a man knitting a shell funeral band. To the extent that *Dead Birds* has a story line, it is the accident of the sequence of events during five months in 1961. But if Gardner had not had the overall story line, he would still have had a film of several reasonably complete shorter event sequences.

12. Whole Bodies

One of the most entrenched conventions of American cinema is the full-face close-up, in which a person's head or even just a face fills the entire screen. The close-up is remarkable on several grounds, the first of which is its unnaturalness. In normal interaction a person may focus visually on another person's face, but only if the two faces are very close to each other will the face be the *only* thing present in the total visual field. Even in cultures where normal conversational distances are relatively short, the eyes of a normally sighted person can visually attend to more than just the face of another by means of peripheral vision and quick eye shifts. A close-up shot of a face does not permit this. As an extreme example, when two people are in sexual embrace, their faces may be so close that their actual visual fields approximate that of a cinematic close-up shot.

But interestingly enough, in such scenes in films where close-ups of faces might be experientially real, close-ups are rarely used, and the camera stays far enough removed to get at least full head-and-shoulder shots. One can accept the proposition that close-ups are perceptually and logically unnatural, but the fact is that they are conventions of film, accepted and expected by filmmakers and film viewers alike.

The real question here must concern their effect on the ethnographicness

TABLE 3.12 WHOLE BODIES

Excessive fragmented close-ups		*Maximally necessary whole bodies*
The Nuer	Dead Birds	Dani Sweet Potatoes
Holy Ghost People		Dance and Human History
		Trance and Dance in Bali
		Dani Houses

As a general rule, long camera shots that include whole bodies of people in frame are preferable on ethnographic grounds to excessive close-ups of faces and other body parts. An occasional close-up that shows otherwise obscure detail is useful, but most ethnographic films thoughtlessly overuse the close-up shot. Among the few films that resist the abuse of the close-up and tend to keep actors in full frame are *Trance and Dance in Bali* and *Dani Sweet Potatoes,* both filmed by anthropologists. Alan Lomax's *Dance and Human History* analyzes dance and work movement, establishing the theoretical basis for the imperative of whole bodies.

of a film. We begin with the obvious fact that every close-up frame of a face means a frame omitting the rest of the body. What, then, are the gains and losses of this particular selection? One argument in favor of close-ups is that they create visual variety and so sustain the viewers' interest. But this argument is based on the assumption of fairly low audience commitment, and I think that it is worth trying to encourage a new way of seeing ethnographic film.

A second argument in favor of the close-up is that film should be allowed to examine parts of a body, or whatever, one after the other in close-up detail in the way that a written account does. But this argument misses the point of a difference between words and film. In order for words to describe an entire body at once, they must move to a very general level. No single word or phrase can describe the details of hands, face, body, and voice. Rather, each must be dealt with in turn, as a kind of isolating close-up. But a film image does hold so much information that a long shot of a person's body can, in fact, allow the viewer to observe hands, face, body, and voice in simultaneous interaction.

A third, more important argument is that full-face close-ups allow the audience to experience and relate to a person. This assumes that the core of the persona is best visible in the face and can be understood through the face. If this is valid, it depends on the fact that the close-up cuts out everything but the face and is not based on the absolute size of the image of the face. Films using facial close-ups are viewed on screens and television tubes of widely varying sizes, with viewers sitting at various distances from the image. So the actual size of a face's image, measured in degrees of retinal image, varies greatly from that for a person who sits close to the screen in a large theater to someone who sits across the room from a small television set. There is certainly some perceptual principle at work here, but I know of no studies of it. I think that it is clear that size of image is less important than limit of information. Close-ups are a convention not because greater size of facial image is desirable. On naive grounds, one might say that if that were so, people would sit in the front of movie theaters rather than toward the rear. Instead, close-ups are used because they concentrate attention on the face and give relatively greater detail. But what is lost when the bodies are omitted? A great deal. It is clear that from an ethnographic standpoint much specific communication is done through the body, and much general cultural information is contained in body movement.

Research on nonlexical or nonverbal communication has shown the importance of the body in modifying, supplanting, and even contradicting those purely verbal messages that had so long been the sole focus of interpersonal communication research (cf. Condon and Ogston 1966; Ekman and Friesen 1969a, 1969b; Birdwhistell 1970, 173; Bateson 1972, 228–243; Davis 2001–2002; Jablonko 2001–2002). Ironically, the loss of communicative behavior through the use of facial close-ups is a relatively small loss in most ethnographic films, since so few even attempt to capture interpersonal communicative behavior.

But the loss of whole body movements in general is important. Alan Lomax and his associates at Columbia University, who carried out choreometric research on dance and work motion, showed that there are definable styles of motion that vary from culture to culture and from culture area to culture area. Lomax's research made us aware of the profound cultural significance of movement itself and what can be called the cultural integrity of the whole body. The implications for ethnographic film are that the entire body must be observed and photographed and that filmmakers must be exceedingly cautious about moving closer than whole body shots (Lomax 1973; Bishop 2001–2002).

There are countless examples in ethnographic films where the camera moves in on faces (or isolates other body parts) and prevents us from seeing what is happening in the rest of the body. In *Holy Ghost People,* a film about an Appalachian Pentecostal church, there are frequent scenes where people enter ecstatic trance states. Their ecstasy is obviously felt and expressed in their entire bodies, yet the camera compulsively zooms in on faces. In *Desert People* and the other films of that series, the facial close-ups prevent us from following the rhythm of whole bodies and even, at times, from seeing the technology of what the whole bodies are doing. The loss of this information is hardly compensated for by the close-ups of expressionless faces, often shot from above so that we do not even have a good view of the face itself.

In *The Nuer,* some of the most effective scenes are long shots of people walking alongside their cattle. One is able to see the exotically graceful ways in which these tall, thin people walk and how their walking seems so in harmony with the movements of their cattle. But in the same film we are not allowed to watch the movements of women pounding maize in wooden mortars as the women stand, rhythmically thrusting the long wooden pestles into the mortars. After a brief establishing shot, the camera plays in and out on moving body parts: upper arms, breasts, and faces. The camera creates its own vision. It is reminiscent of filmmakers who use footage of childbirth or other real events to create a personal aesthetic pattern. This approach can result in an interesting film, but it makes little sense to judge such a film by the standards of ethnographic reality.

It is probable that the information loss is not so critical when the people and the activity in the film are familiar to the audience. Then viewers can reconstruct entire acts from minimal cues. But for most ethnographic films that show exotic acts from exotic cultures, viewers need all the information they can get, and the deprivation of information in the close-up is particularly felt. A counterargument could be made to the effect that the increased detail of a close-up shot of a face gives more information, not less, and in addition, creates a mood of intimacy between viewer and subject that is lost when the camera stays back at the necessary distance to capture images of whole bodies. Although these counterarguments are interesting, they do not seem convincing. But certainly the whole matter should be investigated by empirical research.

The question comes down to this: Is the ethnographic filmmaker to focus on the events of the film or on the conventions of the cinematography? It is very difficult for a creative filmmaker to resist the conventions of the craft. But respect for the subject demands a limit on such conventions and creativity. The words "creativity" and "imagination" must not be allowed to become points of false debate, however. The creativity and imagination essential to good science, here including ethnographic film, are significantly different from the creativity and imagination essential to good art, here including most other uses of film.

It is not possible to make absolute rules like "whole bodies must always be in frame" or "close-ups are always bad." But generally speaking, close-ups should be avoided unless they really contribute to picking out details that are lost in the whole, and then close-ups should be preceded and followed by contextualizing whole shots. This principle holds for close-up shots of technical processes as well as of body parts. I do not want to condemn all close-up shots, but I do want to insist that the close-up should be seen as an extraordinary step, taken only because of extreme necessity. A nice illustration of this turned up in two 30-minute videotapes shot by two students for an ethnographic film course at UCLA in 1974. The subject of both tapes was the same: a father helping his four-year-old son assemble a jigsaw puzzle. Both filmmakers had the same goal, which was to show the interaction between father and son. One tape showed both actors in full frame throughout; the other moved in and out, to the father's face, then to the boy's face, then to the boy's hands, and so forth. The second tape was more aesthetically pleasing, but the first showed much more about the interaction. Filmmakers judged the second more interesting and complained at being asked to watch through a stationary lens for thirty minutes. Anthropologists judged the first more revealing about the father-and-son interaction. Both, in their own terms, were right.

The concepts of "contextualization" and "whole bodies" are different ways of getting at the ability of film to present simultaneously occurring events simultaneously, allowing the viewer's eye to travel back and forth, examining parts and the whole. Word descriptions may attempt this holism, but it is hindered by the inexorable linearity of words strung together in sentences.

13. Whole Interactions

One of the most consistent absences in ethnographic films is any description of communication or other sort of interaction between people. In part this is because normal, naturally occurring conversation is so hard to film. It is a relatively low-energy, fragile sort of behavior, which is easily disrupted by the camera. It is much easier to film one person or many people engaged in some physical activity. So the percentage of real interaction in any ethnographic film is very low.

And when filmmakers do shoot conversation, they usually ignore the more basic fact: conversation is interaction. The work of Gregory Bateson, Ray Birdwhistell, and others, such as Adam Kendon, has clearly shown that a conversation between two people is not just a sequence of utterances. Rather, both parties are communicating constantly about a variety of things. At any one moment, a person may not be speaking words but is nevertheless contributing to the interaction. This is ignored in the usual film or television drama, where conversations or interactions are often filmed as an alternating series of full-face shots of people talking and reacting. In drama this technique may have its uses: by reducing the communication to a minimum, all

TABLE 3.13 WHOLE INTERACTIONS

Including all parties to interaction in frame	Cutaway shots alternating between two parties in interaction	Little or no interaction between people
The Hunters	Farm Song	Dani Houses
Chronicle of a Summer		Dani Sweet Potatoes
Dance and Human History		Dead Birds

It is notoriously difficult to capture face-to-face interaction onscreen. Even in acted fiction feature films where directors have control over their actors, American films make use of cutaway shots, whereas East Asian films are more likely to include both or all parties in the same frame.

attention is crudely and powerfully focused on verbal and (occasional) facial channels. But of course it results in the loss of the great range of communication nuance of real life.

Alan Lomax once pointed out how well the richness of this range is captured in a final sequence in *The Hunters,* where one hunter relates the story of the hunt to others of his camp (pers. comm.). The camera keeps its distance, so not only can we see the vivid act of storytelling, but we can also appreciate the dynamic role of the audience. The giraffe hunt itself is a lonely business, and the four hunters rarely interact. But the climax, the end of that whole act, is a flurry of interaction, and Marshall spends time showing us how the meat is shared and how the stories are told. A strikingly similar scene was used twenty-five years earlier in the Eskimo film *Wedding of Palo,* when Samo tells a group of people how he chased and killed a polar bear. One could argue that both these scenes are too visually complex to be understandable. Indeed, it is only after repeated viewings in slow motion that one can really appreciate the complex coordination of narrator and audience.

One of the few attempts to make a film about a conversation is John Marshall's Kalahari film *A Joking Relationship.* The entire fifteen minutes of the film show the casual banter between a man and a girl. The two are relatives, and their relationship is such that they are not permitted to marry, but they are allowed an informal, even bawdy "joking relationship" (L. Marshall 1957). This film is an extremely interesting attempt to capture the mood of this particular kinship tie, and thanks to a good sound track and subtitles, it is quite effective. But through most of the film the camera moves back and forth in a series of close-ups. Only rarely are the two people shown at the same time. We see one person and then the other. In fact, we hardly see a relationship in the literal sense. The behavioral interactions were created in the editing room. The film is a testimony to how much skillful editing can gild over faulty camerawork.

14. Whole People

It is safe to say that all ethnographic films show people, even though few of the films are actually about specific individuals. But the extent to which individuals are identified and shown as well-rounded personalities varies greatly. Some films show only faceless masses, while others make the viewer acquainted with one or two individuals. There is no single ethnographic standard. Although the goal of ethnography is some sort of generalized cultural or social statement, there are many different strategies of research and description. This is reflected in ethnographic films made by ethnographers themselves. Some, like Adrian Gerbrands's *Matjemosh,* show us much about the life, the work, and even the thoughts of one New Guinea wood-carver. The film is similar to Gerbrands's book (1967), which explores Asmat art through a detailed description of six different carvers. At the other extreme, we find Brian Weiss's *The Turtle People,* shot while Weiss was doing research for his dissertation in ecological and economic anthropology at the University of Michigan. Weiss's film very much reflects his concern for the impersonal impact of outside economic factors on the culture and the society of the Miskito Indians of Nicaragua. Now, one could argue that *The Turtle*

TABLE 3.14 WHOLE PEOPLE

Only faceless masses		*Develops feeling for an individual*
Hanunoo	*Dani Houses*	*Nanook*
The Turtle People	*Dani Sweet Potatoes*	*Dead Birds*
India's Sacred Cow		*Eduardo the Healer*
		I Love You
		Matjemosh

Although the printed word inclines written ethnography toward generalization, the specificity of film makes it easy and desirable to show a few individuals as whole people with real personalities, rather than merely members of faceless masses. *Matjemosh, Dead Birds,* and *Nanook* all explore cultural phenomena by focusing on the lives of one or two individuals. There are rarely advantages in shooting only faceless masses, but for a film like *India's Sacred Cow*—a theoretical statement concerned with the many uses of the cow—specific individuals are less important.

People is just as humane as *Matjemosh* in terms of being concerned with real problems of people. But its strategy is not to focus on any individual Miskito. Films made by nonanthropologists are as varied along this dimension as are those made by anthropologists. However, there is the strong Flaherty tradition of building a film around a single person. Robert Flaherty began this with *Nanook* in 1922 and followed it through his other films. However, the more I see *Nanook,* the less I feel that the film really tells us much about Nanook as a whole person. Perhaps much of *Nanook*'s reputation came from a few shots where Nanook engagingly smiles or laughs into the camera lens. But despite these reservations, there is no question that Flaherty led both naive audiences and film critics to relate directly and warmly to the Eskimo man as a whole person.

So there is precedent in both ethnography and ethnographic film for a wide range of treating or ignoring individuals. But I think that we can argue, as much on filmic grounds as on ethnographic grounds, for whole people rather than faceless masses.

15. Distortion in the Filmmaking Process

It is inconceivable that an ethnographic film could be made in such a way that it did not distort or alter or select its images of reality in a myriad of ways. Therefore it gets us nowhere to ask if a film is subjective or if it distorts reality. The answer to both questions has to be yes.

And as we discussed in chapter 1, ethnographies also distort reality in many ways. One could make a strong argument that because both films and ethnographies do distort reality, there is no point in discussing reality or truth at all. This argument may have a beneficial effect in freeing cinema-as-art from false constraints. But here we are talking about cinema in the service of science. Social scientists (and even physical scientists) are well aware of the distortions and the subjectivity and the selections that enter their research. But at the same time, the scientific goals are phrased in terms of truth or, at the very least, truths; and scientists speak without embarrassment of the possibility of being more or less accurate. Because of this, the nature of a review of a monograph in *Science* is very different from that of a film review in *Film Quarterly*.

This book is to some extent a treatise on the curious relationship of the scientist to truth. As we explored the implications of ethnographic film in chapter 1, we began to look at truth and distortion in an unusual light.

Now I will reformulate the position of this book. I start with the assumption that the task of ethnography is to achieve a truthful and realistic descrip-

TABLE 3.15 DISTORTION IN THE FILMMAKING PROCESS

Time		
Temporal sequences rearranged	*Condensed time*	*Real time*
The Hunters	*Dani Houses*	*The Path*
Dead Birds	*Dani Sweet Potatoes*	*An Ixil Calendrical*
Forest of Bliss		*Divination*

Continuity	
Single sequences constructed out of shots from many actual events	*Actual sequences preserved*
The Hunters	*An Ixil Calendrical Divination*
Dead Birds	*Dani Sweet Potatoes*
The Path	*Dani Houses*

Time, continuity of action and place, and perspective are just some aspects of reality that may be intentionally altered in the process of shooting and editing film. For convenience, we can talk about these in terms of only two variables, time and continuity. Some films are high on one but low on the other, like *The Path,* which presents the Japanese tea ceremony in real time but does so by using shots that were made separately and then edited together for continuity. *An Ixil Calendrical Divination,* on the other hand, was made in real time and shot at a single divination ceremony.

tion and analysis of cultural and social behavior, and I assume that this task is within the reach of a normal ethnographer. It follows that ethnographers attempt to achieve this in their work and that critics base their judgments on the notion that truth and reality are achievable. Although there are many different sorts of ethnographic approaches, each has its own criteria for truth and realism, and therefore each can be carried out more or less adequately.

In other words, ethnography gives us many ways to get at truths and realities. But the acceptance of many ways and many truths and many realities does not mean that everything is equally true. It means that for each of the ways there are truths and nontruths, realities and unrealities. This is basically a position of broad-minded dogmatism.

Selection and omission in the filmmaking process. The filmmaking process is one of tremendous selectivity. A camera is basically just a small box with a hole in one side, through which light passes to register an image on videotape or film. Where the camera is taken, where it is set up, in which direction it is pointed, when it is turned on—all are decisions that form the first stage of selection. Then, in editing, another series of selections are made.

These are all decisions that must be made fairly deliberately, and they result in a film that includes some behavior and omits other behavior. In all this, of course, film resembles ethnography.

In the following sections we will discuss the various sorts of distortions that are found in ethnographic filmmaking, and we will try to evaluate the degree to which these distortions threaten the integrity of an ethnographic film. I have chosen the word "distortion" with due thought and some trepidation. Obviously, the word is not used in a totally negative sense. It is meant to denote all the alterations in the representations of reality that take place during the translation of behavior from original occurrence to the final image on the movie screen.

There are two main sorts of distortions: one occurs when filmmakers, intentionally or inadvertently, cause alterations in the behavior they are filming; and the other occurs during the filmmaking process itself, through the selective acts of shooting or editing.

A. INADVERTENT DISTORTION OF BEHAVIOR

Many ethnographic films purport to show naturally occurring behavior. All ethnographic films have used cameras that are visible and thus intrusive into the behavioral space of the people being filmed. Only rarely have ethnographic films been made of people for whom camera and film crew are a natural part of their behavioral space.

There is the paradox.

In any ordinary ethnographic research, ethnographers can only guess at the effect their presence has on the behavior being observed. They can never observe it in their own absence. In ethnographic film this bind is writ large because the camera is often wielded by a stranger, perhaps assisted by a film crew, and so is far more obtrusive than a single ethnographer poking about, notebook in hand, making observations and interviewing people. Few ethnographers have ever tried to answer the question of the effect of their own presence. It is one of the conventions of anthropology that we usually ignore it.

In fact, only recently have ethnographers made much more than the obligatory acknowledgment that they were there. In his famous introduction to *Argonauts of the Western Pacific* in 1922, Bronislaw Malinowski insisted that ethnographers must explain how they gathered their data. This seems like a minimal demand, but forty-five years later, David Maybury-Lewis, in the introduction to his *Akwe-Shavante Society*, could still regret that "anthropologists are frequently reticent about the circumstances of their field work" (1967, xix).

Actually, while the manner of obtaining data is relatively easy to describe,

TABLE 3.15A INADVERTENT DISTORTION OF BEHAVIOR

Extreme	Moderate	Minimal
	Dead Birds	Les maîtres fous
		Dani Sweet Potatoes
		Dani Houses

The presence of a camera team is bound to have some effect on behavior. No matter how unobtrusive the filmmakers attempt to be, there will be some inadvertent effect on the behavior. The two major factors in this inadvertent distortion are the degree of camera consciousness, resulting in unease before the camera, and the relative energy levels of the camera crew and the subjects. The possession ceremony in *Les maîtres fous* or the battles and funerals in *Dead Birds* had such high levels of energy of their own that the filmmakers were virtually ignored.

Athough the activity in both *Dani Sweet Potatoes* and *Dani Houses* was at a comparatively low energy level, the people were not at all camera conscious, and they were so familiar with the filmmaker that there seems to have been little inadvertent distortion of behavior. It would be possible to use footage of such distortion and incorporate it into a film so as to make a telling ethnographic point. But when distortion is unintentional, uncontrolled, and unincorporated into the ethnographic understanding, it detracts from the ethnographicness of the film.

the extent to which the data reflect the intrusion of the ethnographer is much harder to determine. Ethnographers can write around their presence, creating a conventionally fictionalized account of events that might be called "the ethnographic absence" (a permutation of the phrase "the ethnographic present," referring to another convention of ethnography, in which we describe cultures not as they are but as they presumably existed in some untouched primal state). But even though the ethnographer can write in the mode of "the ethnographic absence," an ethnographic filmmaker usually cannot, because the camera uncompromisingly records the effects of the intrusion and film audiences can easily sense mugging and other forms of camera consciousness.

How does filming affect behavior? Only a few anthropologists have even considered the problem in print. Margaret Mead, writing about the study that she and Gregory Bateson carried out in Bali in 1936–1938 and that involved extensive still and movie photography, suggested that the presence of the cameras had little effect on the Balinese: "They were unself-conscious about photography, accepting it as a part of a life which was in many ways always lived on a stage" (1970, 259). Bateson, writing specifically about still photography (in Bateson and Mead 1942, 49), discussed the factors "which contributed to diminish camera consciousness in our subjects." But these are denials of influence and not real considerations of the extent of the influence. And in fact, in many scenes in the Bateson and Mead Balinese films, especially those showing casual family interaction in a courtyard, the adults do seem to be acting in reference to Bateson and Mead and even appear to be asking them for instructions.

Adam Kendon and Andrew Ferber came to similar conclusions in their study of greeting behavior, where they had set up three 16 mm movie cameras at an outdoor birthday party near New York City. On the basis of the participants' reports and their own observations, they felt that the people were "almost completely unaffected by the cameras" (1973, 598).

But the opposite opinion is stated by Edmund Carpenter. He describes an experiment with natives of the Sepik River area in New Guinea. He first used a hidden camera to film people who were unaware that they were even being observed; then he made them camera conscious and filmed them in that state. Carpenter claims that the presence of the camera totally altered their behavior: "Almost invariably, body movements became faster, jerky, without poise or confidence. Faces that had been relaxed froze or alternated between twitching & rigidity" (1972, 138).

Anthropologists who use film to record and analyze body movement, or nonverbal behavior, often use an interesting argument to support the position that cameras have no significant effect on behavior. They claim that they are looking at patterns of behavior that have been so thoroughly learned and are so unconscious that they will not be easily altered, or if they are altered, the alteration is only on a surface level and does not affect the basic cultural movements.

But these arguments would concern only the most overlearned and unconscious aspects of behavior. To draw an analogy to language is appropriate here. It is one thing to suggest that a person who knows that her speech is being recorded will not make significant changes in her vocabulary, pronunciation, or grammar, but it is quite another thing to say that the content of her speech is unchanged. And in the behavior that is recorded in ethnographic film, what is being done is quite as important as how it is being done.

Pat Loud, the mother and wife in the television series *An American Family,* described vividly how her family altered its behavior at the first suggestion that they would be filmed:

Immediately the Heisenberg Principle—anything observable is changed by the fact of being observed—went into effect and we all became charming, amusing, photogenic, and generally irresistible. We did our number . . . it might not be apparent . . . , but we always put on a good front. . . . We were quite capable of keeping up a running ho-ho banter which perfectly achieved its aim of hiding anything either of us felt about anything. (Loud and Johnson 1974, 89)

You can't forget the camera, and everybody's instinct is to try and look as good as possible for it, all the time, and to keep kind of snapping along being active, eager, cheery, and productive. Out go those moments when you're just in a kind of nothing period, hibernating until you move onto the next thing. (Ibid., 102)

It is interesting to compare Pat Loud's "native" account with that of Alan and Susan Raymond, who shot most of the film for *An American Family* (1973). The Raymonds make no attempt to evaluate the effect of their presence on the Loud family and indeed show no awareness at all that they had any effect. How can we judge these contradictory claims? We have no comparable "native" statements for any other ethnographic film. In the case of *An American Family,* it is clear that at least one subject felt that the film account of her life was wildly inaccurate, while the filmmakers felt that it was accurate. There are obvious possibilities for bias in both accounts. We can take the easiest (but long-delayed) first step and raise the question of the effect of camera intrusion on behavior. The next step, answering this question, is much harder but should be attempted.

Incidentally, camera consciousness may be as hard to simulate as it is to avoid. In Alfred Hitchcock's *Rebecca,* there are scenes of home movies that the characters played by Laurence Olivier and Joan Fontaine took of each other on their honeymoon. In the film as a whole, both Olivier and Fontaine give outstandingly convincing performances, but in this film-within-a-film sequence, neither can capture the easily recognizable symptoms of camera consciousness. They are simply too much in control of themselves.

Relative energy level. A major determinant of disruption is the relative energy level of the event being filmed and the filmmakers. In the Hauka ceremony possession scenes of Jean Rouch's *Les maîtres fous,* or in the funeral and battle scenes of *Dead Birds,* the activity itself had such high energy that it absorbed all the attention of the people, and the cameras were ignored. Kendon and Ferber are quite explicit about this factor in their discussion of camera consciousness at the birthday party, where they claim that "the event gathered its own momentum and proved to be absorbing enough for both adults and children for them not to care very much about the filming" (1973, 598).

But typically in shots of casual activities, where not much is happening and the energy level is comparatively low, attention is drawn to the camera. Then the camera crew becomes a significant part of the total behavior. Often, camera consciousness is marked by people making eye contact with the camera. But there is a subtler form, marked by body stiffness and "unnatural" movement, which audiences can sense even when they cannot precisely describe the cues they have observed.

Mugging. A more extreme sign of intrusion is mugging, a stylized performance in which people interact in exaggerated manner with the camera, making silly faces and gestures. Every photographer has had experiences with subjects mugging in this way. It is a sign of extreme unease at being confronted, not with a familiar human face, but with a glass-and-metal contraption. Mugging may be a kind of exaggeration of gesture into which a person intuitively feels pushed in order to communicate through the opaque barrier of the camera machinery. As shouting is an exaggerated voice level necessary to span physical distance, so mugging is exaggerated nonverbal communication necessary to span the machine-created distance.

Photographic sophistication. In a few cases, camera consciousness has been minimal simply because the people do not know what a camera is. These naive situations are rare and will soon be nonexistent except for very young children. In 1961, when *Dead Birds* was being filmed in West New Guinea, the Dani had had no experience with cameras, and we did not explain what cameras were, since we felt that there was a danger that they would misunderstand and feel threatened. Later, as I came to know the Dani better, I realized that this was an unnecessary fear. But in 1968, when I visited the Dani, I left a Polaroid camera with a missionary, who proceeded to use it quite openly. As a result, by 1970 most Dani in that area were extremely camera conscious and mugged at the sight of a camera. Despite this, a Japanese-Indonesian television crew that filmed the major pig feast in 1970 (see K. Heider 1972a) found what we had experienced nine years earlier: when important ceremonies were going on, the Dani completely ignored the cameras. But today tourists who visit the Dani meet professionals who demand money for posing for photographs.

B. INTENTIONAL DISTORTION OF BEHAVIOR

Nanook's igloo is the classic case of a filmmaker altering material culture. Flaherty found that a normal Eskimo igloo was simply too small and too dark to allow him to shoot inside it. His solution was to have the Eskimo build a half-igloo shell, twice normal size, in which he could show Eskimo home life. This was deliberate distortion done to achieve reality. The film is able to show something of Eskimo life inside the igloo. We see the family un-

TABLE 3.15B INTENTIONAL DISTORTION OF BEHAVIOR

Extreme	Moderate	Minimal
The Path	Dead Birds	Dani Sweet Potatoes
Netsilik series		Dani Houses

The behavior shown in a film may have been intentionally altered or distorted by the filmmaker in a wide variety of ways, ranging from altering the material culture to staging, triggering, or reconstructing behavior. One can speak of this as a variable running from extensive to minimal intentional distortion of behavior, but it does not necessarily correlate with ethnographicness. There can be good ethnographic justifications for any degree of such distortion. One cannot say that the Netsilik Eskimo films, with their reenactment of Eskimo life, or The Path, in which the Japanese tea ceremony was filmed bit by bit, are less ethnographic than Dani Sweet Potatoes, which was filmed with no intentional distortion of behavior. In each film, distortion was made or avoided for legitimate ethnographic reasons.

dressing, getting under the fur covers, going to sleep, and waking. It is hardly a comprehensive treatment, but this is really the only sequence in which the whole family is established as a family unit. The drawback, however, is that we are given a false impression of the size of the igloo living space. And we are given a false sense of the inside temperature when we see Nanook and his family strip off their clothes when it is obviously cold enough for their breath to condense. But Flaherty decided that the advantages of distortion outweighed the disadvantages.

But there is a second decision: Should the filmmaker reveal such artifice, and how? On the whole, filmmakers are reluctant to discuss this, except informally. From an ethnographic standpoint, however, we must know in considerable detail what distortion occurred. To a great degree the ethnographic integrity of a film depends on the extent to which we can learn of the distortions. It is certainly difficult both to create artifice and to reveal it in the course of a film. In most cases it is sufficient to describe it elsewhere, in writing. For example, many of Flaherty's distortions are now well known from the books and articles written about him and his films. But most other reconstructed films, such as the Netsilik Eskimo series, the American Indian series, and the Desert People series, have fallen far short in desirable explanation of how they re-created behaviors and artifacts.

Reality can be deceptive too. Ronald Rundstrom (pers. comm.) has described how the carnations in the teahouse in The Path were chosen and arranged carefully by the filmmakers and the tea mistress to enhance the autumnal mood of that particular tea ceremony. But somehow, perhaps because of the color balance of the film or the wide-angle lens, in the finished film the carnations are too obtrusive.

Interruption of behavior. The filmmaker may interrupt behavior, breaking its flow in order that cameras may be moved, so as to get a variety of shots from different angles. Then the footage can be edited together to create an even flow. In *Dead Birds,* for example, during a minor curing ceremony a man makes a feathered reed wand and gives it to two boys, who run shouting out of the compound. The boys are seen from inside the compound running out, and then the next shot they are shown outside running down The Path. Gardner stopped the boys as they got outside; then he set up his camera outside and filmed them as they resumed running. It would be difficult to argue that this made any significant change in the boys' running behavior.

On the other hand, in *The Path* each shot was set up separately for optimal camera angle, and then it was rehearsed and shot. The filmmakers believed that the women had so routinized their movements after years of training that they could resume the flow of action at will. However, the filmmakers acknowledged that their approach eliminated the easy social chatter that accompanies the movements. Knowing this, the viewer can study the film for its description of movement and gesture but is warned not to use it to study the tea ceremony as social interaction.

The use of two cameras can get around this problem. *Tidikawa and Friends,* made by Jeff and Su Doring in New Guinea, is one of the rare ethnographic films that has used two cameras to good effect in the field. One memorable scene of a man felling a large tree cuts from a close-up of the falling tree to a long shot, leaving no doubt that two cameras were covering the same event. The major drawback, of course, is that the effective use of two cameras creates a larger and more intrusive film crew.

"Staged" behavior. Casual critics of ethnographic films often condemn a film on the grounds that some scenes are "staged." By this they seem to imply that because the behavior was directed by the filmmaker, it is not accurate. This is in fact a very complex question. To evaluate "staged" behavior, we must know the circumstances of filming and the culture being filmed.

There are two related questions: If the events in a film were not purely spontaneous, then what was the role of the filmmaker? And if the events were in some manner instigated or encouraged by the filmmaker, were they events in the current cultural repertory, or were they revived after more or less long abeyance?

Although these facts should be part of the public record of any film with scientific pretensions, they can be established for only a few ethnographic films, and then more often from external published account and oral tradition (i.e., rumor or gossip) than from evidence within the film itself.

Wedding of Palo is a good example of such knowledge, because we know that it is a scripted, acted Inuit love story. But it was directed by Knud Rasmussen, a knowledgeable Arctic anthropologist and traveler whose mother was Inuit, and it was acted in Greenland by Inuit. One scene is of a song duel between Palo and Samo, rivals for the love of the girl. The song duel is a classic conflict-resolution institution, well known from the literature on the Inuit. On these grounds, one can say with fair confidence that the song duel in *Wedding of Palo* is accurate both in its particulars and in its context. But of course that particular song duel never happened. And it is inconceivable that a naturally occurring song duel could have been filmed in anything approaching the detail of that one.

At the other extreme, *The Sky Above and the Mud Below,* a popular travelogue from the 1960s about a trip across New Guinea, was noteworthy for its obvious manipulations and exaggerated claims. For example, in an early scene the camera is traveling up a river in the Asmat and suddenly meets a huge war party of Asmaters in dozens of canoes bearing down on it. Only the most credulous viewer could believe that it is accidental. Obviously the "war party" was arranged for the film. Illegitimate? Not completely, for these *are* Asmat warriors, paddling in the Asmat manner.

Soon thereafter we witness an Asmat initiation ceremony. But it is one that had not been performed for years and was revived for the benefit of the film crew—apparently the roof of the house was even removed to provide enough light for the filming. However, this ceremony is done by Asmaters and must be to some extent genuine. The trouble is that most viewers cannot separate the genuine from that which was dictated by the French film crew.

The behavior in the Netsilik films is also a puzzle. We know that an ethnographic present of 1919 was re-created in the 1960s. It is easy to see how artifacts can be reconstructed from drawings. But how is a complex process like hunting or fishing or housebuilding reconstructed? How much came from the actors' memories, how much from their parents' memories, and how much from Rasmussen's writings? These are the sorts of things we need to know. They are described briefly by Balikci and Brown (1966).

Triggering behavior. Another practice similar to reconstruction is that of triggering the behavior. This is a matter not of reviving some behavior from the past but of influencing the timing for some behavior in current usage.

Bateson distinguished between photographs that are posed and those taken when the ethnographer merely triggers the behavior:

> In a great many instances, we created the context in which the notes and photographs were taken, e.g., by paying for the dance or asking a mother to delay the bathing of her child until the sun was high, but this is very different from posing photographs. Payment for theatrical performances is the economic base upon which the Balinese theater depends, and the extra emphasis given to the baby served to diminish the mother's awareness that she was to be photographed. (Bateson and Mead 1942, 50)

With this distinction, Bateson was trying to make the point that some distortions are good (or at least acceptable) while others are unacceptable. But the matter is much more complex, and it depends greatly on the sorts of data to which one is referring. To evaluate how justifiable it was, we need to know what role the filmmakers played and just how they distorted, or "created the context" of, an event. But even more, we need to have some evaluation by the ethnographer of the result of that distortion. For example, in *Desert People* the opening titles tell us that the film was made of an Australian Aborigine family that had been on a mission station for only three months when it agreed to return to the Western Desert to work with the film crew. That is important and necessary information. But there is no hint whether this might have had any effect on the family's behavior. Were they hunting for food, or were they hunting animals for the camera and then having bully beef with the film crew? And if the latter is true, did it make any difference?

In the middle of filming *Dead Birds,* the leaders of one Dani sib said that they would like to perform the *wam kanekhe,* a renewal ceremony for their sacred stones, but unfortunately they did not have enough pigs; however, if we would pay for the necessary pigs, they could perform the ceremony and we could see it. We paid, they performed, and we watched and filmed. I am still not fully certain what was really going on. We did contribute to the ceremony. But were they planning it anyway and saw an opportunity to make us donate pigs for it? Had our expressed interest in seeing their sacred stones planted in their minds the idea of killing two birds with one set of pigs? As the ethnographer, I should know, but I do not. However, I have no reason to suspect that our role in the ceremony significantly altered the performance of the ceremony as seen in the film or on the level I was able to describe it. (If I had reached a deeper command of the Dani language and culture by that point and had been making a careful study of ceremonial exchange, the data would have been anomalous, with pigs coming from the expedition and not from other particular Dani.)

I feel hesitant about writing about this incident, partly because I cannot give a satisfactory account of all its subtle complexities, and partly because I am sensitive to the persistent rumors that we instigated war among the Dani. We did not, but the rumor is more interesting than the denial and will undoubtedly persist. That is the problem about even describing the circumstances of this ceremony. It is liable to be misunderstood and turned into a claim that we paid for ceremonies. This is at best a partial truth, falsified by being stripped of its context. But it must be discussed, for the question of intervention is one that faces many ethnographic filmmakers and, indeed, many ethnographers. It is important to understand and describe these situations.

A similar situation lies behind the scenes of the *gar* initiation ceremony in *The Nuer,* according to Robert Gardner (pers. comm.). George Breidenbach was alone with the Nuer when an initiation took place, but he was unable to film it because his camera batteries were not charged. Later, the Nuer told him of two more boys who should have been initiated, but because of the disruption of a smallpox epidemic, there was not enough beer available to hold a proper ceremony. Breidenbach offered to supply the beer, and the two boys were initiated. Unfortunately, because of his lack of understanding of the ceremony, the scenes are very incomplete. But there is no reason to doubt the integrity of what he did shoot, since it agrees well with Evans-Pritchard's description of the initiation.

C. EXPLANATION OF DISTORTIONS

Most films that show reconstructed or reenacted behavior simply present it straight as an unacknowledged sort of ethnographic present. Only a very few films indicate in an introductory title or the narration that the behavior is reconstructed. But of course even when this is said, all it does is to serve notice that something is wrong. There is a certain amount of verbal tradition floating around the ethnographic film world—usually misinformed—describing how the scenes were made. It is paradoxical that one can learn more about the technical illusions of feature films, whose purpose is illusion, than about manipulation of reality in ethnographic films, whose purpose is reality.

The Moontrap is a remarkable film because it shows not only the reconstruction event but also the process of that reconstruction. One of the filmmakers, Michael Brault, had worked as cameraman on Jean Rouch's *Chronicle of a Summer,* and *The Moontrap* reflects and extends Rouch's vision of reality in film.

TABLE 3.15C EXPLANATION OF DISTORTIONS

No acknowledgment in film or in print	Some attempt	Fully adequate
The Hunters	Dead Birds	The Path
Dani Houses		Jero Tapakan films
Dani Sweet Potatoes		Forest of Bliss

In the course of filmmaking, a vast number of changes, intentional as well as inadvertent, are wrought on reality. Some of these are quite necessary, desirable, and intentional, others not so. But it is crucial to the ethnographicness of a film that they be explained, justified, and evaluated. This criterion could well be taken to ridiculous extremes: it would be impossible to explain every frame of every shot. But the filmmakers and ethnologists should spell out in reasonable detail how they made the film. The bulk of this has to be done in print, through something like an ethnographic companion or study guide that can accompany the film. The fullest example of this explanation and evaluation is *The Path,* which is accompanied by a detailed publication written by the filmmakers themselves (Rundstrom, Rundstrom, and Bergum 1973). *Dead Birds,* with its ethnographic companion (K. Heider 1972a), is fairly well analyzed from this standpoint, while *The Hunters, Dani Sweet Potatoes,* and *Dani Houses* have fewer printed materials.

We are told in the opening titles of *The Moontrap* that the National Film Board camera crew encouraged the people of a small French-Canadian community on an island in the St. Lawrence River to revive their custom of trapping beluga whales. The film follows one man as he tries to organize the whale trapping. He discusses it with men who were old enough to have participated in it forty years earlier; he searches the town archives for records of how the task was organized; the matter is discussed at a town meeting; and outlines of the last whale trap are located in the river mud at low tide. The idea of the enterprise begins to have a life of its own. The great virtue of this approach is that it does much more than show how some people once trapped whales. It does that, of course, but it also shows the meaning of the past for the present.

The Moontrap has the best of two worlds: It records in detail an interesting and unusual technological process of the past (a film of the same villagers repairing their television sets would not have been as interesting or valuable), and it manages to show how that technological process is embedded in its social context. The film cannot recapture the social context of the original whale trapping, of course, but it does follow out the reverberations of the effort to revive the whale trapping in personal, political, and even religious terms. It was on this score of contextualization that the Netsilik Eskimo films were weakest, for although they also showed old technology, it was re-created for the camera and not placed in the real context of the community. And so despite many nice moments of interpersonal interaction, the Netsilik films are primarily films of individuals-cum-technology, not of technology in context. Of course, the filmmakers of *The Moontrap* were working more or less within their own (French-Canadian) culture, a culture that has changed much less in forty years than most cultures about which ethnographic films are made. But nevertheless, *The Moontrap* is one important model for what ethnographic films can achieve.

Technical distortions created by the filmmaking process. Many sorts of distortions, selections, and omissions arise out of the basic technical steps of shooting and editing. The optics of the lens has an effect on perception of size and distance. For example, even though Robert Gardner filmed most of the battle scenes in *Dead Birds* with normal-focal-length lenses, they had the effect of foreshortening the scene, and so the front lines appear to be much closer to each other than they actually were. What are the ethnographic implications of this? Certainly Gardner's film sequences give a feeling for the movement of Dani battle that neither Matthiessen (1962), Broekhuijse (1967), nor I could capture in words. Yet our printed words are carefully cho-sen, and if they fall short of the film's holistic immediacy or fail in other ways to communicate what we mean, at least they are not betrayed by mechanical effects like the foreshortening distortion of a camera lens. The solution is not to reject film but to understand the distortions of cinema and make the necessary perceptual adjustments. A book like this cannot teach the reader to be able to correct for shots made with different kinds of lenses, but it can alert the reader that lenses distort visual reality in certain specific ways. And, even more important, written material accompanying films can specify where special effects, like telephoto lenses, have been used.

Editing for continuity. One of the most common conventions in film is to edit together shots of a single person or event that were taken at different times and places, in order to create the illusion of real continuity. My favorite example of this is the chase scene in *The Third Man*. The chase takes place in the old inner city of Vienna, where the chaser often loses his man as he cuts around a corner, finds him again, and then catches up, until finally the man disappears (into a sidewalk advertising kiosk, we learn later). The pacing of the scene is excellent and builds up excitement. However, I saw the film after I had lived in Vienna for a year, and it was a thoroughly disconcerting experience. Since street locations were chosen for the photogenic character and cutting was done without regard for geography, people race down one street, turn a corner, and are magically transported to another spot a mile away. Obviously *The Third Man* was edited for drama, and it cannot be used to make an accurate street map of Vienna.

But when this technique from fiction film is carried over into ethnographic film, it is not so harmless. Since we view ethnographic film as much for its true information as for its entertainment value, it does matter whether the continuity of a sequence is real or has been contrived in the editing room.

Ethnographic films contain countless scenes that have been created through editing. For example, when Nanook reaches his igloo in the blizzard and crawls inside, shots of a normal-sized igloo in a blizzard are followed by shots of the mock-up, half-shell, extra-large igloo taken on a clear day.

The giraffe hunt in *The Hunters* is edited together from scenes shot in different years with different men. If audiences could distinguish individual Bushmen—or even different giraffes—the effect would not be possible.

The major battle sequence in *Dead Birds* is put together from shots of different battles at different locations. Also, in *Dead Birds,* scenes of women going to the brine pool for salt alternate with scenes of men at battle, but in fact the brine trek was shot on a different day. All these are examples of distortions, but in each case editing is used to construct a description that is plausible. Before creating the counterpoint of men's battle and women's salt trek, Gardner was careful to determine that it could have happened. And it accurately illustrates the apparent indifference with which women did go about their normal activities while their men were engaged in battle.

This is a good moment in the argument to think some more about the nature of truth in ethnographies and in films. When I wrote the following sentence, I said relatively little, but what I did say was true: "Dani women never approach a battlefield, and in fact often work in the gardens apparently unconcerned, only occasionally looking up when a particularly loud cry comes from battle" (1970, 111). If Gardner as a filmmaker wants to say the same thing in the visuals of a film, he is likely to have to say a great deal more, and not all of it can be literally true in the same sense. The women did go to the brine pool; the men did fight in several battles. But when he edits the footage from several battles together in order to say visually something like "This is what Dani battle looks like" or "This is the best picture I can give you of Dani battles," he follows the convention of filmmaking and lets the narration say, in effect, "This is one battle." So of course the audience sees it as one battle.

Then, he edits battle shots alternating with salt trek shots to communicate visually the idea that while Dani men fight, women do things like getting salt. But again, he follows film convention and claims in the narration that, on the day when that battle took place, these women went to the brine pool—and the audience sees it as an account of one particular Dani day.

Dead Birds is a particularly good film to use for this discussion because Gardner is so talented and knowledgeable as both a filmmaker and an ethnographer that we can assume he knew what he was doing. In his attempt to use the standards and conventions of both cinema and ethnography, he had to compromise, and he betrayed both to some extent. Now we can understand better what he did: in order to capture so many truths about the Dani, he had to tamper with the literal chronological truth in some points. But before we take a purist position, it would be good to recall the discussion in chapter 1 about such cinematographic conventions in juxtaposition to the very comparable distortion that occurs in written ethnography.

Perhaps as we become more aware of these implications, some anthropologists will come to reject ethnographic films like *Dead Birds* in favor of more modest and literally true films like *Dani Sweet Potatoes*. This would be a shame, for the films in the grand tradition have their value as ethnographic and human documents. But we do have the right to insist that, if they are to be taken seriously as ethnography, their distortions must be explained and justified in separate written documents. The ethnographic companion to *Dead Birds* (K. Heider 1972a), written by Gardner and myself, was a step in this direction but has long since gone out of print. I have mentioned above two more recent attempts to address this problem: a monograph on the Jero Balinese films (Connor, Asch, and Asch 1986) and the shot-by-shot discussion of *Forest of Bliss* by Gardner and Östör (2001).

Real time and film time. Another common distortion in film is condensed time. Practically never does film time equal real time except, of course, within each individual shot. The actual time may be indicated visually or verbally. For example, in the narration of *Dani Houses,* I mention how long it took to build each structure. In fact, since the Dani work pattern is quite irregular, the time figures mean very little. But when I showed the work print to audiences, they invariably asked for time data. So I provided these data, but more in the interests of relieving audience tension than for accuracy.

Most events shown in ethnographic films simply take too long to show in real time. Two exceptions occur in *An Ixil Calendrical Divination* and *The Path* (about a Japanese tea ceremony), both of which show short events in real time. It is interesting that most unprepared audiences find both films unbearably long, although they are only thirty-two and thirty-four minutes, respectively.

A few films use brief scenes in slow motion, or freeze frames, to point out complex behavior (as in *Trance and Dance in Bali*) or to dramatize a moment (as in *Dead Birds*). But I know of no use of time-lapse photography in ethnographic films (although once Robert Gardner talked about the potential of time-lapse photography in compressing a day's activity in a marketplace into a few minutes of film, in order to show general trends of activity).

16. Culture Change Made Explicit

Today, even if culture change is not the primary subject of printed ethnographies, it is at least explicitly acknowledged. It is generally recognized that cultures change, and that all cultures change all the time, even though different aspects of cultures change at different rates, and some aspects may even be remarkably stable. Earlier films went to great lengths to preserve or reconstruct a sort of "ethnographic present"—the presumed untouched state before outside influences came in. But this was always an "ethnographic fiction." Nothing illustrates this point better than the contrast between John Marshall's first and last films. In *The Hunters* (1957), the Ju/'hoansi hunt with metal arrow points, and in one scene a hunter wears rubber flip-flop sandals. But the narration ignores these signs of change, and only the most acute observers will notice them. At the other extreme, Marshall's last film, *A Kalahari Family,* is all about the changes that have reshaped Ju/'hoansi life over the last decades of the twentieth century. There are no hints of change in *Dead Birds,* and in my own Dani film, *Dani Sweet Potatoes,* I include a scene where a man splits firewood with a metal ax and I remark on it in my narration. But I make no attempt to analyze the change from stone to steel axes, even though that was going on in front of me. Today ethnographic films routinely deal with culture change.

TABLE 3.16 CULTURE CHANGE MADE EXPLICIT

Timeless "ethnographic present"	Acknowledgment of culture change	Analysis of culture change
Dead Birds	Dadi's Family	Trobriand Cricket
Dani Houses	I Love You	A Kalahari Family

Although cultural change is always going on, it is possible to avoid it altogether in a film. Recent films tend at least to recognize change. In *Dadi's Family,* the grandmother talks about changing family roles even as she resents what is happening to her. *Trobriand Cricket* focuses on how the English game has been changed to fit the Melanesian culture.

ADDITIONAL PRINCIPLES

Particularizing and generalizing. One of the greatest differences between words and pictures lies in the fact that words are necessarily abstracted, generalized representations of reality, whereas photographs, despite the subjective selection involved in shooting, are in some sense direct, specific representations of reality. Not only do ethnographers use words, but they also use words to make generalizations, to state cultural norms. However, the strategy of ethnography is to begin with the data of specific behavior and to move to the cultural generalization. And a good part of any ethnographic writing is description. It is in the realm of the critical anecdote, or the illustrative case, that film most often serves ethnography. Film shows a specific event, carefully chosen and edited for its ethnographic import, and put into a generalizing framework by a few words printed in a title or read in the narration.

So most ethnographic films make cultural generalizations by showing a particular event or artifact or person and implying or openly claiming that the particular is typical, that is, general. Thus, in *Dead Birds* we are invited to see Weyak and understand "adult Dani men"; we see Weyakhe's funeral and understand "Dani funerals." Whether this is a justified step depends greatly on the filmmaker's understanding of the culture and the filmmaker's skill at choosing shots that are indeed fairly typical. But obviously behavior varies so much that no one man or single funeral can really be representative of all men or all funerals. The ethnographic filmmaker has an obligation to select reasonably representative events, but also to provide, perhaps in the film and certainly in supplementary written material, those ethnographic data that will spell out the relation of the specific image to the range of variation of those specifics and to the general.

These thoughts raise an interesting question: How far *can* films go in making general statements out of specific raw material? It is obvious that this can be done with generalizing words read in a narration. But how much can it be done visually?

Douglas L. Oliver, in his monograph on the Siuai of Bougainville, said that his photos would give a better idea of Siuai physique than his words could (1955, 10). So ethnographic films that show dozens or hundreds of people in a society can provide the raw materials for generalization. In *The Nuer* this is done quite deliberately in several sequences that show a dozen or more short shots of ivory bracelets, tobacco pipes, or scarification designs. Thus, although one photograph or twenty-four photographs per second can never actually make a generalization, a film can show a range of acts, events, or artifacts and so set up a generalization. In terms of film language, or the semiotics of film, we can think of two sorts of visual implications or statements. In one, a single representation is shown and a generalization implied—for example, "This is how Weyak behaves and therefore how Dani men behave." In the other, we see many different representations, and the implied statement is "Here is how so many hundred Dani men appear, and therefore this is the range of similarity and variation of Dani men."

For the most part these unspoken "statements" are merely filmic implications and are not really comparable to explicit, mutually understood intentional linguistic utterances. To some extent the filmmaker intended to make them, and to some extent some viewers perceive them, but there are always ambiguities: one can legitimately ask, "What did he say?" and "Is that what he really meant?" Such ambiguity may be used to great effect in art, and, indeed, it may be considered the essence of art. But it is not tolerable in science. So we must insist that ethnographic filmmakers clarify in narration or in writing the extent to which they mean generalizations to be made.

One of the films in the Desert People series (part 2, *Gum Preparation, Stone Flaking; Djagamara Leaves Badjar*) does this well, taking particular pains to warn us when it would be false to draw the logical generalization from the visuals. At the beginning' we are told that the films were made in an unusually dry spell, certainly an important factor on the Western Desert of Australia. Elsewhere we see a man perform a task but are told that usually women do it; we see a bark dish but are told that most dishes are made of solid wood; and as we see a man getting gum from grasses, we are told that this time he is having particular difficulty in making the gum congeal.

Semiotics. "Semiotics," or "semiology," is a general term for a wide range of interests that have developed out of linguistic concerns. One of these interests concerns the way in which cinema resembles language. A language is a system of symbols used to communicate; a film uses symbols to communicate. But the crucial semiotic question focuses on the "system": Does a film or do films embody regular systems that are in any sense comparable to syntax or lexica? Put another way, do the concepts of syntax and lexicon help in understanding film? The idea is fascinating, but I do not intend to deal with it at any great length here. Much of this work has been done in French and is only gradually being translated (e.g., Metz 1974).

Sol Worth, in his 1969 paper "The Development of a Semiotic of Film," explores these sorts of questions: Is there a grammar of film; if so, is there a possibility of "ungrammatical" film statements? But Worth is careful not to claim too much. The experiment with Navajo filmmakers that Worth carried out in collaboration with John Adair attempted to explore some of these implications: If there is something analogous to a language of film, will Navajos make films in some sort of Navajo film language that is different from other (English, Hollywood, etc.) film languages?

As yet, there is very little in the way of results that one can point to with any degree of confidence. At present the differences between film and the language of ordinary discourse seem more important than the similarities: language is a more precise, instrumental medium of communication; film communicates, of course, but in a more diffuse, noninstrumental way. The utterances of language are brief, and reaction and correction are immediate, usually measurable in seconds; with film, if there is any comparable message turnaround time, it is measured in months and years. Film may be more analogous to novels or plays. But even there, while novels and plays are constructions of the language of everyday discourse, the ingredients of film (shots and sequences of shots) are not present in ordinary discourse of any sort.

Despite these problems and uncertainties, we can point to some general principles.

1. Cutaway Shots

The juxtaposition of two shots often implies that the contents of both are related. When a shot of a face watching something off-camera is followed by a shot of a logical something, it is almost inescapable that the filmic statement be read as "X is watching Y." A very common cinematographic technique using this type of juxtaposition is the cutaway, when shots of an event are broken by close-ups of people's faces supposedly watching the event. The cutaway has special perils for ethnographic film.

First, the cutaway is often used to break up a long action, on the assumption that the audience cannot tolerate focusing its attention on a single act for more than a few seconds. But in fact it is more likely that in ethnographic film we need to see a long and uninterrupted act and that the editor's decision to cut away will be based on some arbitrary number of seconds and will do violence to the integrity of the action. (A slightly more excusable use of the cutaway is when the camera has stopped or run out of film, and the cutaway is a sort of rescue operation.) This of course rarely happens with video, where a single take can last an hour or more.

Second, the shots inserted as cutaways are usually shot before or after the main action. Then, when they are inserted into the sequence of an action, they are likely to be misleading. If the main action is a vehement speech or the peak moment of a funeral, for example, we understand the cutaway to mean something like "This is how X was observing and reacting to this moment in the speech or the funeral." Such cutaways could be literally true if two cameras were being used in synchrony with each other. If not, the cutaway is more or less false. It has only aesthetic rationale and adds nothing of ethnographic value. I would go further and say that the ethnographic demand for a longer, uncut shot would be more aesthetic, despite its cinematographic unconventionality.

2. Camera Angle

A very common practice is to shoot downward on people. In my experience most ethnographic filmmakers are taller than most people being filmed. When cameras are handheld or tripods are set up, the camera is usually at comfortable standing height for the filmmaker, but, especially in close-ups, this results in the camera and the viewer looking down on the people. Now, one can talk about the meaning of camera angle. Specifically, let us imagine three close-up shots of a person, showing just head and shoulders: one at her eye level; one from above, looking down on her face; and the third from below, looking up into her face. Each of these three shots would have somewhat different connotations. One of the important dimensions of meaning that vary here has to do with superiority/inferiority, status, and personal distancing. Of course, the English words appropriate to the situation reinforce this suggestion: specifically, that a shot from above, or a film that consistently shoots from above, is in some way making the viewer superior, looking down on the people who are beneath him. This is one factor in what can be called the semiotic of film. It seems certain that continuous use of high camera angles results in greater distance and less empathy and thus perverts what is presumably one goal of ethnographic film.

3. The Audience

Intended audience. Printed anthropology is generally written with a specific audience in mind: reports of research and theoretical contributions are presented in journal articles and monographs aimed at professional colleagues; textbooks, prepared for students, are secondary reworkings of description and theory; and occasionally anthropologists write popular accounts in such journals as *Natural History* or in books aimed at a general lay audience. These are not absolute categories, for journal articles are reprinted in readers for courses, and monographs may be also used in courses; an occasional textbook like Eliot D. Chapple and Carleton S. Coon's *Principles of Anthropology* (1942) may also be an important theoretical formulation; and series like the Holt, Rinehart, and Winston Case Studies in Anthropology, edited by

George and Louise Spindler, were short ethnographies written for classroom use and may be the only comprehensive reports on particular cultures. But on the whole, writers have fairly specific ideas of their primary audience and adjust their writing to the appropriate level.

Most ethnographic films, on the other hand, seem to have been made with little thought for any specific audience. The outstanding exception is the Netsilik Eskimo films, which were carefully designed for a primary-school audience. During the planning stages a team of educational specialists, led by psychologist Jerome Bruner, worked out a program for using ethnographical materials to introduce basic social science. They decided on the specific concepts they wanted to communicate to a specific audience and then produced films that would best accomplish this.

Film demands on the audience. The range of demands that film can make on an audience is nicely demonstrated by the old and new versions of *Nanook.* Flaherty originally made *Nanook* with various visual puzzles that first heightened the awareness of viewers as they tried to understand what was going on and then rewarded them by showing the outcome. The revised version of *Nanook,* however, introduces explanatory narration and soothing music. Viewers now are disengaged and merely relax in the wash of sight and sound. There is little left to be attentive to. The narrator attends to all.

We have already discussed how easy it is to overload a film with so much information that viewers simply cannot comprehend it all. The most obvious sort of overloading is to read great quantities of information in the narration.

Another way to overload a film is to lead viewers to a level in the action that is simply too complex to be grasped in a film. The Marshall Kalahari film, *An Argument about a Marriage,* is overloaded in this way. If viewers were only to see the film as an argument, there would be no problem. But the filmmakers wanted to make the viewers understand the historical background and present course of a fast-moving argument involving the complex Bushman marriage practices. No viewer can keep up. Film simply cannot carry so much information. Even if a film is designed for a high level of complexity, there are bound to be questions that can be answered only in written accompaniments.

Perhaps *The Path* makes more demands on an audience than any other ethnographic film. It was designed not just to describe the Japanese tea ceremony but also to reproduce its qualities so that audiences could use it almost as a meditation or a study experience. At the other extreme, Flaherty made his films for a general theater audience and probably had no thought that one day they would be seen almost exclusively in classrooms. The Bateson and Mead Balinese films are the closest approach to a filmic monograph, and certainly they were conceived as an integral part of a monographic report.

But for the most part, ethnographic films apparently try to appeal to all audiences. (One must say "apparently" because the filmmakers' aims are rarely accessible.) There are some advantages to this approach. It does give a film a chance at several different markets. But this advantage may be illusory. In fact there is basically only one market for ethnographic films: the educational or classroom market. This market uses films as much for entertainment value as for informational, educational value. There is a sort of positive feedback at work. Films are entertaining, so they are used for entertainment. And so most anthropologists have not considered the serious anthropological potential of film. (An important exception to this is in the study of primate behavior. Since E. R. Carpenter's films of monkeys in the 1930s, primate films have been important scholarly productions.)

It is probably fairly easy for filmmakers to state, if pushed, the audience they had in mind for any particular film. But I think that for most filmmakers this is an ex post facto rationalization. To the extent that they have an audience in mind, it is a select preview audience of their friends.

A more interesting question concerns the attributes of ethnographic films that are made for entertainment or for instruction. The major differentiating dimension is the intensity of information. Films like *Nanook* and *The Nuer* contain relatively little information but give much atmosphere; films like *Childhood Rivalry in Bali and New Guinea* and *Dani Sweet Potatoes* are loaded with information and spend little time on pure atmosphere.

In my experience of showing ethnographic films to schoolteachers, I have been surprised at the resistance to films that show "naked savages." Nakedness is culturally patterned, of course. The Dani are extremely modest, in the sense that they do have some body parts that must be covered, and they are quite embarrassed if these should inadvertently be exposed. But to most American audiences, bare breasts of mature women or scrotums of mature men constitute nakedness. And schoolteachers strongly resist using films that show peoples whose patterns of body coverage differ from their own. The teachers say that their pupils are too immature to see such films without making jokes or that the parents would object. As an anthropologist, I accept this as an accurate appraisal of at least parts of contemporary American culture. It is undoubtedly very fortunate, and perhaps no accident, that the major curriculum film project for grade schools was made on the Netsilik Eskimos, a fully clothed people.

Credibility. For me one of the most baffling and subjective attributes of ethnographic films is credibility, or believability. For years I have been showing ethnographic films to audiences of many different sorts, and I am still surprised at what people will or will not accept. Much of the narration in *Mosori Monika,* which was shot in Venezuela, comes verbatim from statements made by a Warao Indian woman and a missionary nun. These statements were translated into English and read by people with slight accents. Chick Strand, the filmmaker, obviously tried hard to create a sense of the two conflicting realities, that of the Indians and that of the missionaries. But to my surprise, many viewers think that the entire narration was created out of Strand's imagination.

A somewhat more understandable but equally unjustified disbelief greets *The Turtle People.* The beginning titles establish the Miskito Indians as living in Nicaragua. Most viewers know that Nicaragua is Spanish-speaking, but practically none know that the Miskito actually speak English, not Spanish. So when we hear heavily accented English in a first-person native narration, it is difficult to believe that it is genuine. Perhaps in these films some explanatory introductory titles could help—if people would believe the titles.

Earlier, I questioned the convention of the ethnographic present in ethnographic films. But for some viewers this convention allows them to believe. Many viewers are disturbed by the asphalt highway that appears in the background of some shots of Peter Furst's *To Find Our Life: The Peyote Hunt of the Huichols of Mexico.* In fact, the Huichols do now use vehicles in their peyote quest, and some of their sacred spots are beside highways. It would be much more logical if Furst's honesty had strengthened the credibility of his film, not weakened it. In reporting these reactions, I may seem to undermine the previous arguments for explicit reality. Of course that is not my intention. In fact I have no idea how representative are the doubters I reported on, and I should expect that, as viewers become more sophisticated, their credulity will become better placed.

THE ATTRIBUTES AS DIMENSIONS

The previous discussion has treated a number of principles that underlie any consideration of the ethnographicness of film. These attributes can now be considered as continua or attribute dimensions, along which the various films can be placed. Although it would not be sensible to treat any of the attribute dimensions as finely calibrated scales, it is possible to present them as qualitative scales. But the purpose of the attribute dimensions is to present a systematic way of analyzing any ethnographic film, and I hope that the reader will not hesitate to use the attribute dimension diagrams as a sort of notebook or tally sheet on which to enter comments on other films, whatever their ethnographicness. Diagram 1, below, provides a convenient form for this.

Diagram 1. The attribute dimension grid

1. Appropriateness of sound	
2. Narration	
3. Ethnographic basis	
4. Explicit theory	
5. Relation to printed materials	
6. Voice: point of view	
7. Holism: behavioral contextualization	
8. Physical contextualization	
9. Reflexivity: the ethnographer's presence	
10. Whole acts	
11. Narrative stories	
12. Whole bodies	
13. Whole interactions	
14. Whole people	
15. Distortion in the filmmaking process	
15a. Inadvertent distortion of behavior	
15b. Intentional distortion of behavior	
15c. Explanation of distortions	
16. Culture change	

MAKING ETHNOGRAPHIC FILM

This book is more about the ethnographicness of films than about films in general. Likewise, this chapter contains thoughts about how to make films more ethnographic, and it does not attempt to cover all aspects of filmmaking. The basic technology of filmmaking is the same for all films, however ethnographic they attempt to be. This technology can be learned in cinematography classes, and some people can do much learning on their own with the help of excellent recent books on filmmaking (e.g., Barbash and Taylor 1997).

THE ETHICS OF ETHNOGRAPHIC FILMMAKING

The making of an ethnographic film raises extraordinarily complex ethical questions. Especially since the mid-1960s, anthropologists in the United States have been attempting to spell out in some detail their ethical responsibilities. This is difficult enough for ordinary ethnographic research; for ethnographic filmmaking, it is almost impossible.

As far as I know, the Society for Visual Anthropology has never attempted to draft a code of ethics specifically for visual anthropology or to guide ethnographic filmmaking. (And I have served on its board of directors and as its president.) However, the latest version of the Code of Ethics for the American Anthropological Association is available on the AAA website (www.aaanet .org). It has been revised several times over the decades but still does not directly address the problems of visual images. The central tenet of the code is that anthropologists should not harm the people they study. However, even this becomes problematic today, when anthropological research, in advocacy of threatened minorities, tries to expose the actions of the threatening powers and thus is critical of one side of the issue (and that side is the one issuing research visas).

A second problem is the requirement for gaining informed consent from all with interests in the research.

These demands seem impossibly stringent. But they are all based on a single underlying imperative: we have a responsibility to do nothing that will harm the people we study and film. The great problem, of course, is to anticipate the potential damage a film might do to people's physical, social, and psychological welfare, as well as to the "safety, dignity, or privacy of the people" with whom we work. The ethnographic filmmaker, as well as the ethnographer, must be aware of the considerable responsibility that accompanies the license to study and to film.

The conscientious ethnographic filmmaker will avoid the more obviously unethical practices. But it really is not possible for people to give fully informed permission for their images to be used in a film. When I was filming the Dani in West Irian in 1963, I made no attempt to explain what films were all about. I simply did not think that it could be done in any meaningful way. In fact, Frederick Wiseman's experiences in filming U.S. institutions turned up quite remarkable evidence that even people in the United States, who are ostensibly highly sophisticated about movies and television, cannot make informed decisions of the sort demanded by the ethics statement.

Wiseman described his procedure in an interview in *Filmmakers Newsletter:* "If anyone objects either before, during, or immediately after a sequence is shot, I don't use it; but I don't give anyone the right of review thereafter" (Halberstadt 1974, 21).

The problem is that at the moment of shooting no one can really know how the footage will turn out or how he or she will appear. And the subject certainly cannot anticipate what will be preserved, omitted, or juxtaposed during the editing. And also it turns out that even when people see themselves in a finished film, they cannot anticipate how that film will affect others. It is especially true with the subjects of ethnographic films, who for the most part have never been in a film before.

This was illustrated by the controversy that arose around Wiseman's 1974 television film, *Primate,* which was about the Yerkes Primate Research Center. In a letter to the editor of the *New York Times* (15 December 1974), Dr. Geoffrey H. Bourne, director of the center, objected to the Wiseman film on the grounds that it "not just distorts the truth but actually inverts it so that the scenes are telling lies." The next week (22 December 1974), Wiseman replied in defense that no one had objected during the filming and that Bourne apparently had had no objections to the finished film until he saw the reviews. (For more on Wiseman and informed consent, see Anderson and Benson 1988.)

The dilemma is evident. If a filmmaker acknowledges an obligation to obtain permission, or releases, from the people in the film, then how can the filmmaker arbitrarily declare that the obligation is fulfilled at the time of shooting and that thereafter the subjects have no more rights? On the other hand, if the subjects exercised rights of review throughout, then few films would ever be finished. This is a complex ethical as well as legal question, and the American Anthropological Association statement on ethics is of little help. As long as the subjects of ethnographic films were ten thousand miles away from the audiences, there seemed to be little real problem. But now that ethnographers are making films in the United States, and people in New Guinea are using films themselves, the situation has changed. I shall not pretend to offer any answers, but I must emphasize that filmmakers should keep these considerations in mind. Ethnography and filmmaking cannot guarantee always to produce studies that are thoroughly pleasing to all involved, but they should at least not be vulnerable to charges of falsification of a situation. The most important introduction to such problems is *Image Ethics,* edited by Gross, Katz, and Ruby (1988; see also Barbash and Taylor 1997, 48–69, and the *Visual Studies* issue devoted to ethics [Papademas 2004]).

AN ETHNOGRAPHIC FILM MUST BE BASED ON ETHNOGRAPHIC UNDERSTANDING

The principle that an ethnographic film must be based on ethnographic understanding is so obvious and fundamental that it is tautological. And yet it is resisted explicitly or implicitly by most cinematographers involved in ethnographic film. I would go further and say that when films are made on subjects of ethnographic concern, the use of ethnographic understandings not only makes films more ethnographic but also makes films better aesthetically.

If a film is to be informed by ethnographic understanding, it is virtually essential that a knowledgeable ethnographer be intimately involved as *ethnographer* in each step of the filmmaking process. It is not enough merely to have a token ethnographer present, perhaps holding a microphone, as was apparently the case with many ethnographic film projects.

The ideal arrangement is for the ethnographer to do the fieldwork first, complete the analysis and writing, and then return to the scene with a filmmaker to shoot a film that has been carefully thought out on the basis of the written work. This course was followed in making *The Feast* and *Kypseli.* After Chagnon had spent two years studying the Yanomamö of southern Venezuela and had written his booklet, he returned with Timothy Asch to film chapter 4 as *The Feast;* after Susannah Hoffman had spent a year studying the Greek village of Kypseli and had completed her PhD dissertation on sex roles in the village, she returned with Paul Aratow and Richard Cowan to film her dissertation. My own films, *Dani Sweet Potatoes* and *Dani Houses,* were shot on my second trip to the Dani, after I had spent nearly two years studying Dani horticulture and construction. After Linda Connor had worked with Jero Tapakan in Bali, she returned to Jero with Timothy and Patsy Asch to make the series of films about the spirit medium. The filmic quality of all these films varies considerably, but they are more ethnographic than any films made only by competent cinematographers could possibly be.

For various reasons, the ethnography and the cinematography may be done concurrently. This is true, for example, of the Bateson and Mead Balinese films, of *Dead Birds,* and of *The Turtle People.* This can be fairly effective and is relatively economical. But in most ethnographic studies, the full implications of the study are not realized until the end of the study or even until the analysis is complete, long after leaving the field. The study can be described quite satisfactorily in sentences forged then. But no new footage can be shot, and a partial salvage job is often necessary—patching over inadequate footage with an informed but ex post facto narration.

The worst cases are the real salvage jobs, where some well-intentioned but ethnographically naive person shoots footage and then brings cans of film to an anthropologist or editor to ask what can be done. Except in the rarest of cases the footage is a total loss.

The saddest cases are anthropologists who have shot film of situations they knew very well, but without thinking in filmic terms, and usually with cameras they had bought in a tax-free shop en route to the field and have had no experience in using—indeed, cameras they haven't even had time to test for mechanical failure. In short, it is not enough that an ethnographer (or an ethnography) be available. The ethnographic film must emerge from the ethnographic understanding. But not all ethnographic insights are equally filmic.

AN ETHNOGRAPHIC FILM MUST EXPLOIT
THE VISUAL POTENTIAL OF FILM

A picture is worth ten thousand words. But not any picture, and not any words. The major conceptual step from ethnography to film is to decide what aspects of the ethnography can be described more effectively in film or which aspects of the verbal description of the ethnography can best be supplemented by film.

The answer is different in each case. As a nice exercise in this sort of thinking, one can take any important article or monograph in the anthropological literature and work out a film that would best enhance these specific written words. One can conjure with all the possibilities of film to show holistic interrelationships of people and landscapes; the infinite nuances of human interaction; styles of expression and movement; ambience, tempo, and feeling of group events; and processes from beginning to end. One can use film of naturally occurring events, acted events, or animation.

WHOLE BODIES, WHOLE INTERACTIONS, AND WHOLE PEOPLE IN WHOLE ACTS

Holism is a useful ethnographic principle for an ethnographic filmmaker. Close-up shots of faces should be used very sparingly, for entire bodies of people at work or play or rest are more revealing and interesting than body fragments. Events should be shown from beginning to end. In *Dani Houses,* I was concerned with showing the entire sequence of house construction. Now, thinking about that film in retrospect, I wish that I had gone on to show how the houses were used. I did show a whole process, and there is a real sense of closure with the last shot of the newly finished house in the late afternoon sun. It is a satisfactory account of a whole act. But I now think it would have been much stronger if I had defined the subject as construction *and* use of Dani houses.

DIVISION OF LABOR

Should one person be both filmmaker and anthropologist? Or should there be a filmmaker in addition to the anthropologist? This is a strongly debated question, and it is usually resolved on the grounds of available financing or other extrinsic considerations. This may be the best way to answer the question, rather than taking a definitive stand on theoretical grounds. I do think that it is unreasonable to expect one person to be able to fulfill the duties of both ethnographer and filmmaker in the field, and it is even harder to do both tasks in the postfield period. In most cases where one person has tried to do both, the ethnography or the film has suffered, or the completion of one or both has been inordinately delayed. The success of teams in making the Netsilik Eskimo films, *Dead Birds, The Feast, Kypseli, Desert People,* and the Balinese films about Jero, to name just a few, supports the argument that one person should be the filmmaker, and another the ethnographer. But it is also essential that each person should understand and respect the métier of the other. This may be the most difficult obstacle to overcome. Jean Rouch (1974) argues strongly against a team on the grounds that the extra people are simply too disruptive of the situation. He favors a single anthropologist/cameraperson assisted by a local person trained in sound operations.

THE MEANING OF REAL COLLABORATION

Hadza is a good example of a film made by a skilled filmmaker and a very knowledgeable anthropologist, but it shows a lack of real collaborative thought. The Hadza are a tribe of hunter-gatherers in Tanzania who, like many such groups, have considerable leisure time. The main activity of the men seems to be gambling. The film includes a long sequence of gambling activity, and the narration explains the rules of the game and the general cultural context of gambling for the Hadza. But the visuals are general shots, and the narration might as well have been written before the footage was shot. They are of the same subject but are not successfully coordinated.

The filmmakers should have phrased their problem in terms like this: What is especially visual about this activity, and how can it best be shown on film? They do show the group of men sitting around the gambling spot, and one man throwing disks against a tree. So far so good. It is a good setting shot, showing whole people. But gambling is surely entertainment and interaction, with winners and losers, involving some emotional investment, some strategies; yet none of this was captured in the visuals. The *Hadza* has achieved a major degree of ethnographicness, not only in the informed narration but also in the way in which the visuals do cover the ethnographically important aspects of Hadza life. But yet it falls short of maximal ethnographic use of film. It was good to say "Gambling is important, so we need a gambling scene." But the next, most creative step was not taken, where the question is "What is ethnographically important and visually accessible?"

We are talking about what might be called an inductive approach: starting with an understanding of the facts and then shooting for them. Certainly the *Hadza* is a far cry from the other approach, which involves shooting for interesting scenes and actions and then putting together some sort of statement. The Jero Balinese films, *The Goddess and the Computer* (also about Bali), and *I Love You: Hope for the Year 2000* are all more recent examples of informed collaboration between anthropologists and filmmakers.

AN ETHNOGRAPHIC FILM
CANNOT STAND BY ITSELF

This axiom may be an affront to a traditional filmmaker, but it is obvious to the anthropologist who has seen and thought about an ethnographic film. An ethnographic film must arise from an ethnographic understanding of a culture, and it can present much at which the words of a written ethnography can only hint. On the other hand, no film can communicate all the information that we can legitimately ask of ethnography. In particular we need to know the circumstances of the ethnographic research and the filmmaking and the cultural context of the behavior, much of which involves generalizations of fact and abstract concepts. These are essentially verbal, not visual. Some sense of them may be printed in titles or read as narration, but only at the risk of detracting from the visual power of the film.

In short, while film can play an important role in ethnographic description, it cannot satisfy all of ethnography's needs. An ethnographic film must be supplemented by written material. Just as the making of an ethnographic film must be one part of an ethnographic research enterprise, so the results must include both film and printed material.

ETHNOGRAPHIC FILMS FROM RESEARCH FOOTAGE

The use of film and videotape records as primary data for anthropological research has only begun. For example, much research on what is loosely called nonverbal behavior requires a microlevel of analysis that can only be done by repeated frame-by-frame viewing. The film itself is then the data and should be published as part of the technical report. However, there are many technical problems that have not yet been overcome in "publishing" film with a journal article.

Ray Birdwhistell made a study of *Microcultural Incidents in Ten Zoos,* and his only report to date is a film made of a lecture presented in 1968 under that title. The film incorporates the original footage, slowed down and repeated where necessary to point out the more subtle actions. Another film, *Invisible Walls,* by Richard Cowan and Lucy Turner, shows the results of a study of proxemics, or personal space. And *Maring in Motion,* made by Marek Jablonko, is a compilation of research footage used by Alison Jablonko in her choreometric study of New Guinea Maring motion. Jablonko's dissertation is available through Xerox University Microfilms (Ann Arbor, Michigan), but neither Birdwhistell nor Cowan and Turner have published the details of their studies. As this kind of research increases, some way must be found to publish the results of both film and articles.

PRESERVATION OF THE FILM RECORD

Footage shot by anthropologists, especially of rapidly changing tribal cultures, represents an invaluable record and source of data that must be preserved for future generations of the subjects themselves and for scientists who will be engaged in research as yet unimagined. Whatever the possibility of this footage as ethnographic film today, it should be annotated and preserved. Film that is lost is irreplaceable. One of the horror stories of anthropology tells of the footage taken by A. L. Kroeber of Ishi, the last "wild" California Indian, in 1914. According to the story, the footage was stored near a heating pipe in the University of California museum and simply baked out of existence. Footage should be stored in a vault with temperature and humidity controls.

But unless the footage is annotated, it is nearly as good as lost. The National Anthropological Film Center at the Smithsonian Institution allows anthropologists and others to deposit their footage, with annotations, in a secure place where others would have access to it.

FIVE

THE USE OF ETHNOGRAPHIC
FILMS IN TEACHING

Most instructors who use ethnographic films at all woefully underuse them. At worst, ethnographic films serve as babysitting devices to fill a few sessions while the instructor is out of town or otherwise disinclined to give a lecture. For the students, film sessions usually result in pleasant experiences in dark rooms, but little more. Even when instructors wish to make good use of films, they rarely have anywhere to turn. The books that they use they have read in advance and can set into perspective, but not so with films. Most film rental contracts are for one showing only, and even if the film is locally owned, the effort of setting up extra screenings overwhelms most teachers. So films are shown with minimal knowledge or preparation and only seen once—unlike a book, which can be read carefully, and parts reread, more or less at leisure. Birdwhistell, in his excellent discussion of this whole problem, recommended a minimum of two preview screenings for each film (1963). But this is hardly ever done, even by the most conscientious instructors. I am not sure whether to be discouraged thoroughly that films are used in such a casual way or to be heartened that, despite so many problems, films are so widely used.

Of course, most of us encounter films almost exclusively in the context of movie entertainment or, in the form of television commercials, as sales propaganda. As a result, we are trained so thoroughly in one mode of seeing that this poses a major obstacle to the use of film in teaching, where the entertainment and propaganda values are less important than the purely informational value. It is much easier for a student to gain intellectual content and stimulation from a book than from a film. And yet, that intellectual content and stimulation are just what we hope ethnographic films can somehow provide.

One purpose of this book is to indicate how to make films that are more ethnographic. And as films become more ethnographic, they will be more usable for teaching ethnography (see also Asch 1974).

FILMS AND BACKGROUND READING

In 1966, I assembled the first edition of the catalog *Films for Anthropological Teaching*. That first edition listed some ninety films. By the eighth edition in 1995 (K. Heider and Hermer), there were more than four thousand titles. Much of this increase represents ethnographic films completed since 1966. The catalog lists film titles, credits, distributors, descriptions, and, most important, a bibliography of related printed materials.

The first requirement for using an ethnographic film in teaching is that the instructor know the film well enough to incorporate it into the course. The instructor should be able to read material about the cultural events depicted in the film and should have seen the film and be able to prepare the class for it. Just as one usually prepares students to read a monograph by alerting them to certain key problems, so can one prepare students to view a film. With printed material, students can always return to it to read for more understanding. This is rarely done with films, although the advantages are strong. Ideally there would be a preparatory lecture, then a first screening, followed by discussion, and then a second screening followed by what would certainly be a much deeper discussion. As long as ethnographic films are merely time-wasting entertainments, real discussions do not take place, and second screenings would be pointless. But when an ethnographic film can be understood, it can be exploited in this way. And, of course, unless it is exploited in this way, it cannot be understood. However, this is not really an unbreakable vicious circle. The key to understanding an ethnographic film, or gaining information from it, is not just repeated viewings but the availability of written materials that can fill in what the film leaves ambiguous.

The catalog *Films for Anthropological Teaching* lists as much as possible of the literature related to each film that will allow classes to understand the film. Unfortunately, few films have anything approaching useful related literature. There are many problems.

For example, *Grass* shows the dramatic semiannual migration of the Bakhtiari herdsmen of Persia. The filmmakers' popular account of their adventure (M. Cooper 1925) is long since out of print, and I know of no ethnographic study of the Bakhtiari that could answer the questions the film raises. The closest is Fredrik Barth's work on similar groups several hundred miles to the south of the Bakhtiari (1961). Another sort of problem is availability: Bateson and Mead wrote an excellent book, *Balinese Character* (1942), which nicely complements their Balinese films, but the book is scarce and expensive and thus cannot be used conveniently for classes.

The Nuer was filmed on the culture that E. E. Evans-Pritchard had studied thirty years earlier, and his books and articles are easily available. In fact, his monograph, *The Nuer* (1940), has been used in paperback edition in classes. But the film is so non-ethnographic that the more instructors know about the culture, the less likely they are to be willing to use the film. I would argue strongly that while the film has many ethnographic shortcomings, it can be used to good advantage. It does capture some of the ambience of a Nuer cattle camp and is an exquisitely beautiful film. It can be seen by students before they read the monograph. One problem with asking students to read technical monographs in classes is that when the culture is too exotic, it is difficult for students to make much sense of the monograph. Seeing *The Nuer* film gives them a kind of holistic impressionistic sense for the Nuer, and so they have some cognitive landscape, someplace to anchor what they read. I would think that the seventy-three minutes spent seeing the film would be worth far more than an extra seventy-three minutes rereading the monograph, in terms of understanding even abstract principles of lineage organization.

The Dani research represents one model. The same events shown in Gardner's film *Dead Birds* and my two short films, *Dani Sweet Potatoes* and *Dani Houses,* are described and analyzed in several books and articles by the various members of the Harvard Peabody Expedition (see Matthiessen 1962; Broekhuijse 1967; Gardner and Heider 1969; K. Heider 1969, 1972b). The most important of these for teaching purposes was a 75-page pamphlet (or module) called *The Dani of West Irian: An Ethnographic Companion to the Film "Dead Birds"* (K. Heider 1972a), which has long since gone out of print. This ethnographic companion is specifically designed to be used by instructors and assigned to students in connection with the film. It includes a 26-page ethnographic sketch of the Dani, more or less a condensation of my 330-page ethnography on the Dani, but with special reference to events shown in the film; an essay by Robert Gardner in which he discusses why and how he made the film; and a shot-by-shot analysis of the 663 shots in the film, printed in double column alongside the narration of the film. And now Gardner has released a DVD on *Dead Birds.*

The purpose of the ethnographic companion is to increase the accessibility of the information of the film. It was really made as an afterthought, when it became clear that something was needed to bridge the gap between our technical writings about the Dani and the film. But now we can expect more and more ethnographic films to be made concurrently with this sort of written accompaniment.

Timothy Asch's work is especially notable here. In all of his projects he played a dual role of filmmaker and teacher, always insisting on having teaching materials to accompany the films.

STRATEGIES

The most common strategy in using an ethnographic film in teaching is to screen the film once, perhaps preceded by some introduction and followed by some discussion. An extremely simple but effective variation is to show the film twice. Because ethnographic films are of such totally unfamiliar subjects, the first viewing tends to inundate audiences with indigestible impressions. The real appreciation and absorption of filmic data increase tremendously with a second viewing. (I am tempted to say "increase immeasurably," but the increase is probably measurable and could be the subject of a useful study in itself.)

Another highly effective use of ethnographic films in teaching is to show a film, or part of a film, without sound and to ask the students to study it as raw data. Archaeologist James Deetz first suggested this to me, and I have subsequently tried it, using a twenty-minute section from *Dead Birds*. First the students see that twenty minutes, without narration, and write down what they think was happening. Then they see the entire film from the beginning, with narration, and once again write what was happening, in the key twenty minutes, paying special attention to how and why they might have been wrong in their first interpretations of the action.

I have tried several variations on Deetz's idea. In 1970, Dani children were playing a game that I called hit-the-stick. I videotaped the game, and now I use a fifteen-minute sequence in class, challenging the students to figure out the rules by studying the behavior. (This illustrates a definition of culture that emphasizes "rules (in peoples' heads) about behavior (on the ground)." In fifteen minutes, undergraduates can, with a bit of prompting, form hypotheses, test them, revise them, and come up with a good set of the rules that these Dani children were playing by (K. Heider 1977).

For American students, Australian Rules Football provides a similar experience. That game is sometimes shown on cable television in the United States. It is a game particular to southern Australia, evoking for Americans images of baseball, football, soccer, volleyball, lacrosse, and rugby. A few students (usually male) have some idea of how it is played, but for most it is just too complex to decipher. And of course the Australian commentators are talking to people who are already in the know, so they go on and on about particular plays but never try to explain the rules.

In the 1950s, Harold Conklin was carrying out fieldwork among the Hanunoo of the Philippines and both filmed and recorded Hanunoo activity. From this he edited an eighteen-minute film called *Hanunoo*. When I first viewed it, I was not impressed, because it was just a series of vignettes with no explanation and no apparent continuity: neither whole acts nor narrative story line. Now I find it useful as a puzzle film. I ask students to watch it carefully, writing down everything that they learn about the people. Even those who have little knowledge of anthropology do surprisingly well with the material aspects of the culture. Then I ask, "What did you not learn from this film?" The answers now cover most of religion, social organization, political organization, psychology—all those more nonvisual aspects of culture (see K. Heider 2004a).

All of these strategies are effective in heightening students' appreciation of film as data. They not only have studied films with extraordinary concentration, but they have also taken an important step toward seeing film in general through more sensitive eyes.

APPENDIX

A Brief Descriptive Catalog of Films

Although this book does not attempt to make a full description or critique of any one film, there are references to many films scattered throughout it. The following is a list of most of those films, with description and bibliography, more or less freely adapted from various sources, especially the catalog *Films for Anthropological Teaching,* eighth edition (K. Heider and Hermer 1995). The catalog itself lists some four thousand titles and is obtainable from the American Anthropological Association (www.aaanet.org).

There are many chances for error in a catalog such as this. Credits are not standardized, and it is often difficult to tell from titles like "filmmaker," "director," "anthropologist," and "producer" just what a person's role in the filmmaking was. Distributors change, and prices rise constantly. And in all too many instances, supposedly authoritative sources give two or three different dates of release and even running times of films. I have listed some distributors, trying in each case to give at least the primary distributor (the source for purchasing prints, tapes, or discs), together with some rental sources. I have not attempted to give purchase and rental prices.

DISTRIBUTORS

AEMS: Asian Educational Media Service, 910 S. Fifth Street, Champaign, IL 61820; www.aems.uiuc.edu

American Friends Service Committee, Program Coordinator, 2161 Massachusetts Avenue, Cambridge, MA 02141; pshannon@afsc.org; www.afsc.org

Artefakt Productions, Neubruckstrasse 80, CH 3012, Bern, Switzerland; znoj@ethno .unibe.ch

B&C Films, 10451 Selkirk Lane, Los Angeles, CA 90024

BM: Berkeley Media LLC, 2600 Tenth Street, Suite 626, Berkeley CA 94710; info@ berkeleymedia.com; www.berkeleymedia.com

C5: Cinema Five, 595 Madison Avenue, New York, NY 10022

CHF: Churchill Films, 662 N. Robertson Boulevard, Los Angeles, CA 90069

Cont/McG-H: McGraw-Hill Contemporary Films, Inc., Princeton Road, Hightstown, NJ 08520; 828 Custer Avenue, Evanston, IL 60202; 1714 Stockton Street, San Francisco, CA 94133

CRM Films, 2215 Faraday Avenue, Carlsbad, CA 92008

DER: Documentary Educational Resources, 101 Morse Street, Watertown, MA 02472; docued@der.org; www.der.org

El Nil Research, 1147 Beverwil Drive, Los Angeles, CA 90035; www-bcf.usc.edu/~elguindi/VisualEthnography.htm

EMC: Educational Media Collection, Box 353095, University of Washington, Seattle, WA 98195–3095; risimiki@u.washington.edu

First Run/Icarus Films, 32 Court Street, 21st Floor, Brooklyn, NY 11201; mail@frif.com

HR&W: Holt, Rinehart, and Winston, Inc., Media Department, 383 Madison Avenue, New York, NY 10017

IFB: International Film Bureau, Inc., 332 S. Michigan Avenue, Chicago, IL 60604

IU: Indiana University, Instructional Support Services, Bloomington, IN 47405; iss media@indiana.edu

MOMA: Museum of Modern Art, 11 W. Fifty-third Street, New York, NY 10019

NYU: New York University Film Library, 26 Washington Place, New York, NY 10003

Phoenix: Phoenix Films, 470 Park Avenue S., New York, NY 10016

PSU: Pennsylvania State Media Sales, 118 Wagner Building, University Park, PA 16802; lxm49@psu.edu

RAI: Royal Anthropological Institute Film Library (rental only within the UK), www.therai.org.uk/film/film.html

RBMU: Regions Beyond Missionary Union, 8102 Elberon Avenue, Philadelphia, PA 19111

SPF: Special Purpose Films, 26740 Latigo Shore Drive, Malibu, CA 90265

Sumai: The Sumai Film Company, Box 26481, Los Angeles, California 90026.

UEVA: Universal Education and Visual Arts, Inc., 221 Park Avenue S., New York, NY 10003

USNAC: United States National Audiovisual Center, Washington, DC 20409

FILMS

An American Family (1973). A twelve-part series produced for WNET (television) by Craig Gilbert.

A dramatic, controversial documentary about a middle-class white family living in Santa Barbara, California. Unique for its length, its intimacy, and its nonexoticness (for the U.S. television audience). A major subject of conversation among intellectuals in the United States during mid-1973. The controversies focused on the filmmaking process and on the nature of the culture depicted. Most viewers had a much better basis for making judgments than they do for most "ethnographic" films.

Goulart, Ron. 1973. *An American family*. New York: Warner Paperback Library.
Loud, Pat, with Nora Johnson. 1974. *Pat Loud: A woman's story*. New York: Coward, Mc-Cann, and Geoghegan.

Raymond, Alan, and Susan Raymond. 1973. Filming an American family. *Filmmakers Newsletter* 6.5:19–21.

The American Indian Series (1961–1965). Includes *Acorns: Staple Food of California Indians; Basketry of the Pomo* (three films); *Beautiful Tree—Chishkale; Buckeyes: Food of California Indians; Calumet, Pipe of Peace; Dream Dances of the Kashia Pomo; Game of Staves; Kashia Men's Dances; Obsidian Point-Making; Pine Nuts; Pomo Shaman; Sinew-Backed Bow; Sucking Doctor; Totem Pole; Wooden Box: Made by Steaming and Bending.* Distribution: Contact http://hearstmuseum.berkeley.edu/collections/main.html.

Made under the anthropological direction of Samuel A. Barrett of the Department of Anthropology, University of California at Berkeley. The project was begun during the 1950s and the films released during the early 1960s. Produced by University of California Extension Media Center. Filmmakers involved included Clyde Smith, William Heick, Ernest Rose, Al Fiering, Cameron Macauley, Robert Wharton, and David Perri.

Most of these films show California Indians, especially Kashia Pomo. The technology films range from fairly narrow reconstructions to broadly conceived holistic accounts (e.g., *Beautiful Tree—Chishkale*). There are four Pomo ritual films. Barrett died before the completion of this project, and extensive ethnographic documentation is not available.

The Anastenaria (1969). 17 min.

Follows the spectacular Christian/pagan spring ritual of Macedonian Greeks. Includes ecstatic trance states and walking on hot coals. The narration gives a heavily analytic (Jungian) interpretation of events.

Appeals to Santiago (1969). 28 min. By Arnold Baskin in collaboration with Carter Wilson, Duane Metzger, and Robert Ravicz. Distributed by EMC.

Follows the "cargo" ritual of the Chiapas (Mexico) Maya, in which different men assume the responsibility of caring for saints' images over the course of a year. Describes the ritual from the Mayan point of view (in contrast to Cancian's economic explanation).

Cancian, Frank. 1965. *Economics and prestige in a Maya community.* Stanford, Calif.: Stanford University Press.

An Argument about a Marriage (1968?). 18 min. Made from John Marshall's footage shot in the 1950s. Distributed by DER.

A dense film that tries to follow an intricate conflict between two groups of Kalahari Bushmen. The first part of the film uses English narration over stills to explain the argument and its historical and cultural context; then the film follows the argument as it developed, using only postsynchronized Bushman voices with English subtitles.

See bibliography for *The Hunters.*
Reichlin, Seth, and John Marshall. 1974. *"An argument about a marriage": The study guide.* Somerville, Mass.: Documentary Educational Resources.

The Ax Fight (1971). 30 min. By Timothy Asch in collaboration with Napoleon Chagnon. Distributed by DER.

Four differently edited versions of a Yanomamö dispute.

Biella, Peter, Gary Seaman, and Napoleon Chagnon. 1997. *Yanomamo interactive: Understanding "The ax fight."* Fort Worth: Harcourt Brace. CD-ROM.

The Baboons of Gombe (1974). 52 min. Made for ABC television by Hugo van Lawick. Distributed by MCA DiscoVision, www.oz.net/blam/DiscoVision/Library.htm (under "Informational").

Focuses on the Beach Troop of baboons on the banks of Lake Tanganyika, at the Gombe Stream Reserve, where Jane Goodall has been studying chimpanzees since 1960. An important sequence shows a newcomer maneuvering for leadership in the troop.

A Balinese Trance Séance (1980). 30 min. By Timothy Asch and Patsy Asch, with Linda Connor. Distributed by DER.

The first of five films about the Balinese spirit medium Jero Tapakan as she performs a trance séance for a bereaved family.

Connor, Linda, Patsy Asch, and Timothy Asch. 1986. *Jero Tapakan, Balinese healer: An ethnographic film monograph.* Cambridge: Cambridge University Press. Rev. ed., Los Angeles: Ethnographic Press, Center for Visual Anthropology, University of Southern California, 1996.

Bitter Melons (1968?). 30 min. One of the later films made from John Marshall's footage shot in 1955 in the Kalahari Desert—perhaps the earliest synchronous sound shot in the field. Edited by Frank Galvin. Distributed by DER.

Focuses on a Kalahari Bushman who composes songs and melodies for the one-string bow. The pieces he plays cover a wide range of Bushman concerns. By the device of starting each sequence with the music in synchronized sound and then cutting to visuals that illustrate his themes, the film itself also covers a wide range of topics in Bushman culture.

See bibliography for *The Hunters.*
Reichlin, Seth. 1974. *"Bitter melons": A study guide.* Somerville, Mass.: Documentary Educational Resources.

Box of Treasures (1983). 28 min. By Chuck Olin and the U'mista Cultural Centre. Distributed by DER.

Kwa Kwaka' Wakw (Kwakiutl) of Alert Bay, Vancouver, held a last potlatch in 1921, but it was illegal by Canadian law, and all the ceremonial goods were confiscated by the government. Finally, in the 1980s, some of the objects were returned to the people, who built a cultural center to hold and preserve them.

Webster, Gloria Cranmer. 1991. The contemporary potlatch. In *Chiefly feasts: The enduring Kwakiutl potlatch,* edited by Aldona Jonaitis, pp. 227–250. Seattle: University of Washington Press.

Candles for New Years (1998). 30 min. By David Plath, with Jacquetta Hill. Distributed by DER.
New Year's celebration in a Lahu village, northern Thailand.

Childhood Rivalry in Bali and New Guinea (1952). 17 min. By Gregory Bateson and Margaret Mead in 1936–1938. Distributed by NYU.
The first filmic attempt to be comparative explicitly. It shows comparable scenes from two different cultures: Bali and the Iatmul of the Sepik River in New Guinea. Uses some naturally occurring similar situations, such as ear piercing, and also "experimental," or created, situations, such as giving a doll to a child to provoke rivalry reactions.

See bibliography for *Trance and Dance in Bali.*

Chronicle of a Summer (1961). Ca. 90 min. By Jean Rouch and Edgar Morin. Distributed by First Run/Icarus Films.
The first synchronous sound, cinema verité film about the attempts of an anthropologist (Jean Rouch) and a sociologist (Edgar Morin) to discover what Parisians were thinking in the summer of 1960. It is mainly talk, with practically no "action." Unsurpassed for self-conscious honesty in showing Rouch and Morin in the film asking questions, influencing events; native feedback when the first version is shown to the people and they respond; and final scenes where Rouch and Morin discuss their achievement.

Freyer, Ellen. 1971. *Chronicle of a summer*—Ten years after. In *The documentary tradition,* edited by Lewis Jacobs, pp. 437–443. New York: Hopkinson and Blake.
Levin, G. Roy. 1971. Jean Rouch. In *Documentary explorations,* edited by G. Roy Levin, pp. 131–145. Garden City, N.Y.: Doubleday.
Rouch, Jean. 2003. *Ciné-ethnography.* Edited and translated by Steven Feld. Minneapolis: University of Minnesota Press.

The Cows of Dolo Ken Paye: Resolving Conflict among the Kpelle (1970). 32 min. By Marvin Silverman in collaboration with anthropologist James L. Gibbs Jr. Distributed by HR&W.
Gibbs's description (from K. Heider 1972, 18–19):

The wounding of a crop-eating cow by a Kpelle farmer starts a dispute which is followed to its conclusion in a hot-knife trial by ordeal. Photographed in Fokwele, Liberia, in 1968, the film shows the conflict as it actually unfolded. Events filmed before the wounding of a cow indicate that the outburst was not random, but rooted in the ways in which cattle are used and in the complex relationships of the

prosperous, cattle-owning chiefs and the ordinary farmers who are their constitu-
ents. Flashbacks of actual events provide historical depth. The actions of the ordeal
operator invite the viewer to consider how supernatural beliefs, physiological processes and applications of psychology all contribute to the working of the ordeal.

This is one of the most conscientious and respectful collaborations between a filmmaker
and an anthropologist who knows the culture intimately.

Gibbs, James L., Jr. 1965. The Kpelle of Liberia. In *Peoples of Africa,* edited by James L.
Gibbs Jr., pp. 197–240. New York: Holt, Rinehart, and Winston.

Dadi's Family (1981). 58 min. By the National Film Board of Canada. Distributed
by DER.
Dadi, Grandmother, manages her extended family in a village in the state of Haryana,
in northern India. A vivid view of family dynamics.

Dance and Human History (1974). 40 min. By Alan Lomax and Forrestine Pauley.
Distributed by DER.
Presenting the results of Lomax's choreometrics research, correlating dance and work
movement with technology.

Dani Houses (1974). 16 min. By Karl G. Heider. Distributed by DER.
Follows the construction process of the two sorts of Dani houses, round and rectan-
gular. Shot in 1963, two years after *Dead Birds,* in the same neighborhood of the Grand
Valley Dani (West New Guinea, now Irian Jaya, Indonesia). An elemental technology
film, made by an anthropologist who had spent two years studying Dani technology.

See bibliography for *Dead Birds,* especially K. G. Heider 1970, pp. 252–272.

Dani Sweet Potatoes (1974). 19 min. By Karl G. Heider. Distributed by DER.
Follows the sweet-potato cycle of Dani horticulture from clearing the gardens through
planting to steaming and eating. Shot in 1963, two years after *Dead Birds,* in the same
neighborhood of the Grand Valley Dani (West New Guinea, now Irian Jaya, Indonesia).
Mainly technology, with some child-rearing sequences.

See bibliography for *Dead Birds,* especially K. Heider 1970, pp. 31–44.

Dead Birds (1963). 83 min. By Robert Gardner. Distributed by DER. (In 2004 the Film
Study Center at Harvard University released a two-disc, special-edition DVD of *Dead
Birds* with many extra features, available through DER.)
A film on some Grand Valley Dani of Netherlands New Guinea (now the Indonesian
province of Irian Jaya), especially Weyak, a man, and Pua, a boy. The structure of the
film follows the events of war and ritual that occurred during the shooting of the film

and utilizes the Dani symbolism of man-as-bird as a metaphor for death. Filmed between April and September 1961 in an unpacified part of the Grand Valley of the Balim River.

Gardner, Robert, and Karl G. Heider. 1969. *Gardens of war: Life and death in the New Guinea Stone Age.* New York: Random House.

Heider, Karl G. 1970. *The Dugum Dani: A Papuan culture in the highlands of West New Guinea.* Chicago: Aldine.

———. 1972. *The Dani of West Irian: An ethnographic companion to the film "Dead Birds."* New York: MSS Information Corp.

———. 1997. *Grand Valley Dani: Peaceful warriors.* 3rd ed. Fort Worth: Harcourt Brace.

Matthiessen, Peter. 1962. *Under the mountain wall: A chronicle of two seasons in the Stone Age.* New York: Viking.

Desert People (1969). 51 min. By Ian Dunlop in collaboration with anthropologist Robert Tonkinson.

This is part 4 of the *People of the Australian Western Desert* series (see below), and the most general film of the series.

Tonkinson, Robert. 1974. *The Jigalong Mob: Aboriginal victors of the desert crusade.* Menlo Park, Calif.: Cummings.

Eduardo the Healer (1978). 54 min. By Douglas G. Sharon, Richard Cowan, Christopher Donnan, and Robert Primes. Distributed by DER.

Tells the story of the life of Eduardo Calderon, becoming a *curandero,* or healer, on the north coast of Peru.

Calderon, Eduardo. 1982. *Eduardo el Curandero: The words of a Peruvian Healer.* Richmond, Calif.: North Atlantic Books.

El Sebou': Egyptian Birth Ritual (1986). 27 min. By Fadwa El Guindi. Distributed by El Nil Research.

El Guindi, Fadwa. 2004. *Visual anthropology: Essential method and theory.* Walnut Creek, Calif.: AltaMira.

Farm Song (1979). Distributed by AEMS. Consultant: John Nathan.

Explores the dynamics of four generations of a Japanese "house" family in northern Japan.

The Feast (1970). 29 min. By Timothy Asch, in collaboration with anthropologist Napoleon Chagnon. Distributed by DER.

An account of the alliance-making gift exchange and feasting between two previously warring villages of Yanomamö Indians, who live in southern Venezuela. The first part of the film is a heavily narrated explanation of what will happen; the main body of the film shows the events of one feast with synchronized sound and an occasional English subtitle. The film was designed to illustrate chapter 4 of Chagnon's ethnography.

Chagnon, Napoleon. 1997. *Yanomamö*. 5th ed. Fort Worth: Harcourt Brace.

Fit Surroundings (1998). 30 min. By David Plath and Jacquetta Hill. Distributed by DER.
   The women who dive for shellfish on the Shima Peninsula of central Japan.

Floating in the Air, Followed by the Wind: Thaipusam (1973). Ca. 33 min. By Gunther Pfaff in collaboration with psychiatrist Ronald Simons. Distributed by DER.
   An account of the Hindu penitential ceremony performed by Tamils living in Kuala Lumpur, Malaysia. To thank the god or to appeal to the god, individuals go into trance, have pins thrust through their skin, or carry burdens anchored by sharpened hooks inserted into their skin and walk to a temple. The film uses footage of interviews with penitents and footage of the actual ceremony.

Forest of Bliss (1986). 90 min. By Robert Gardner in collaboration with Ákos Östör. Dying and death rituals in Benares (Varanasi), India. Distributed by DER.

Gardner, Robert, and Ákos Östör. 2001. *Making "Forest of bliss": Intention, circumstance, and chance in nonfiction film*. Cambridge, Mass.: Harvard University Press.

The Goddess and the Computer (1988). 58 min. By Andre Singer, with anthropologist J. Stephen Lansing. Distributed by DER.
   Lansing establishes that the irrigation systems of Bali are coordinated by Hindu priests and water temples. A holistic approach.

Lansing, J. Stephen. 1991. *Priests and programmers: Technologies of power in the engineered landscape of Bali*. Princeton, N.J.: Princeton University Press.
———. 1995. *The Balinese*. Fort Worth: Harcourt Brace College Publishers.

Grass (1925). 66 min. By Merian C. Cooper and Ernest B. Schoedsack.
   The first part of *Grass* is a banal and dated travelogue. In the second part, the filmmakers follow the Bakhtiari tribe (of Persia) and their herds on their annual trek from their lowland winter grazing grounds to their summer lands, in search of grass. Certainly one of the most dramatic human experiences ever filmed.

Cooper, Merian C. 1925. *Grass*. New York: G. P. Putnam's Sons.

Gum Preparation, Stone Flaking; Djagamara Leaves Badjar (1969). 19 min. By Ian Dunlop in collaboration with anthropologist Robert Tonkinson.
   This film is part 2 of the series *People of the Australian Western Desert* (see below).

Gurkha Country: Some Aspects of Fieldwork in Social Anthropology (1967). 19 min.
By anthropologists John and Patricia Hitchcock. Distributed by PSU.
   One of the rare films about fieldwork. Made by the Hitchcocks about their own
research and living experiences with the Magars of the Nepal Himalayas.

Hitchcock, John T. 1966. *The Magars of Banyan Hill.* New York: Holt, Rinehart, and
   Winston.

Hadza: The Food Quest of a Hunting and Gathering Tribe of Tanzania (1966).
40 min. By Sean Hudson in collaboration with James Woodburn. Distributed by RAI.
   A view of the Hadzas as a hunting-and-gathering tribe that spent a minimum amount
of time in food gathering and had much leisure time to sit around talking and gambling.

Woodburn, James C. 1968. An introduction to Hadza ecology: Stability and flexibility in
   Hadza residential groupings. In *Man the hunter,* edited by Richard B. Lee and Irven
   De Vore, pp. 49–55, 103–110. Chicago: Aldine.

Hanunoo (1957/1993). 18 min. By Harold C. Conklin. Distributed by PSU.
   Scenes from the life of the Hanunóos in southeastern Mindoro, Philippines. Shot by
anthropologist Harold Conklin in 1952–1954.

Conklin, Harold C. 1957. *Hanunoo agriculture: A report on an integral system of shifting
   cultivation in the Philippines.* Rome: Food and Agriculture Organization of the United
   Nations. (Reprinted in 1975 by Elliot's Books, Northford, Conn.)
Heider, Karl G. 2004. An 18-minute trip to the field. In *Strategies in teaching anthropology,*
   3rd ed., edited by Patricia C. Rice and David W. McCurdy, pp. 131–134. Upper Saddle
   River, N.J.: Prentice Hall.

Holy Ghost People (1967). 53 min. By Peter Adair. Distributed by Cont/McG-H; rental
by EMC.
   A view of the white Pentecostal church in Scrabble Creek, West Virginia, whose members enter ecstatic trance, speak in tongues, and handle poisonous snakes to show that
they are possessed by the spirit. Introduced by interview sequences in which the people
describe their behavior and beliefs, then a long, synchronized sound sequence of the
prayer meeting itself.

La Barre, Weston. 1962. *They shall take up serpents: Psychology of the southern snake-
   handling cult.* Minneapolis: University of Minnesota Press. Paperback ed., New York:
   Schocken Books, 1969.
Mead, Margaret. 1968. Review of *Holy Ghost people. American Anthropologist* 70:655.

House of the Spirit: Perspectives on Cambodian Health Care (1984). 43 min. Distributed by American Friends Service Committee and EMC.

Two American physicians learn to take Khmer ideas of health and sickness into account and to work out relations with Krou Khmer, Khmer healers, when treating Khmer refugees in the United States.

How To Behave (1987). 43 min. By Tran Van Thuy. Distributed by First Run / Icarus Films.

A Vietnamese government film crew is challenged to make a film about what real people do and undertakes a very ethnographic-like survey. Whether documentary or scripted, this is a fascinating inside view of culture.

The Hunters (1956). 73 min. By John Marshall. Distributed by DER.

A story about four Kalahari Desert Bushmen and their search for food for their families. After wounding a giraffe with a poison arrow, they track it for days, finally kill it, and bring the meat back to distribute to their people. Essentially a film about the hunting techniques and the hunting knowledge of the Bushmen.

Lee, Richard B. 1969. !Kung Bushman subsistence: An input-output analysis. In *Environment and cultural behavior,* edited by A. P. Vayda, pp. 47–79. Garden City, N.Y.: Natural History Press.
———. 2002. *The Dobe Ju/'hoansi.* 3rd ed. Fort Worth: Harcourt Brace.
Marshall, Lorna. 1965. The !Kung Bushmen of the Kalahari Desert. In *Peoples of Africa,* edited by James L. Gibbs, pp. 241–278. New York: Holt, Rinehart, and Winston.
Ruby, Jay, ed. 1993. *The cinema of John Marshall.* Chur, Switzerland: Harwood Academic Publishers.
Thomas, Elizabeth Marshall. 1959. *The harmless people.* New York: Knopf.
Thompson, William Irwin. 1971. Values and conflict through history: The view from a Canadian retreat. Chap. 4 in *At the edge of history.* New York: Harper and Row.

I Love You: Hope for the Year 2000 (1999). 77 min. By Kathrin Oester and Heinzpeter Znoj. Distributed by Artefakt Productions.

In central Sumatra, Indonesia, a matrilineal Muslim community has weddings only once a year. The films follows the attempts of the anthropologist (as well as the principals) to find out who is going to marry whom, but the families—especially the women—manage to keep it a secret until the last moment.

Znoj, Heinzpeter. 2004. *Heterarchy and domination in highland Jambi: The contest for community in a matrilinear society.* New York: Columbia University Press.

India's Sacred Cow. 28 min. By the National Film Board of Canada.

A compilation film exploring Marvin Harris's thesis that the taboo on killing Zebu cattle in India, far from being a counterproductive religion-driven mistake, makes good sense in ecological terms.

Harris, Marvin. 1979. *Cows, pigs, wars, and witches: The riddles of culture.* New York: Random House.

Invisible Walls (1969). 12 min. By Richard Cowan and Lucy Turner. Distributed by PSU.

A filmic demonstration of the principles of personal space and boundaries, developed by Edward T. Hall under the general label of proxemics. The film shows an experiment carried out in some Los Angeles shopping centers. A hidden camera captures people's reactions to the actors when they move too close, invading the personal space.

Birdwhistell, Ray L. 1970. Review of *Invisible walls. American Anthropologist* 72:724.
Hall, Edward T. 1959. *The silent language.* New York: Doubleday.

An Ixil Calendrical Divination (1966). 32 min. By Carroll Williams and Joan Williams in collaboration with anthropologists B. N. Colby and L. Colby.

Among the Ixil Maya of Guatemala, professional diviners get answers to their clients' questions by laying out beans in a sort of calendar order as they are chanting prayers; this process is repeated again and again. The film uses synchronous sound and, after the introductory shots, shows only the diviner's hands arranging and rearranging the beans, in order to give the ceremony in real elapsed time.

Jaguar (1967). 93 min. By Jean Rouch, Damoure Zika, et al. Distributed by DER.

An exuberant acted account of what might have happened to three youths who make the trip from Niger to Ghana and back.

Rouch, Jean. 2003. *Ciné-ethnography.* Edited and translated by Steven Feld. Minneapolis: University of Minnesota Press.
Stoller, Paul. 1992. *The cinematic griot: The ethnography of Jean Rouch.* Chicago: University of Chicago Press.

Jero on Jero: A Balinese Trance (1986). 30 min. By Timothy Asch, Patsy Asch, and Linda Connor. Distributed by DER together with *A Balinese Trance Séance* (see above).

A Joking Relationship (1962). 13 min. By John Marshall.

Shows the culturally standardized joking relationship between !Nai and her great uncle. See also the entry for *!Nai.*

See bibliography for *The Hunters.*

A Kalahari Family (2002). 6 hr. John Marshall's culminating statement about the Ju/'hoansi of the Kalahari. Distributed by DER.

    Part 1: A Far Country. 91 min.
    Part 2: End of the Road. 60 min.
    Part 3: The Real Water. 60 min.
    Part 4: Standing Tall. 60 min.
    Part 5: Death by Myth. 90 min.

See bibliography for *The Hunters.*

Karba's First Years (1952). 19 min. Made by Gregory Bateson and Margaret Mead in 1936–1938. Distributed by NYU; rental by NYU.

Follows the major developmental stages in the infancy of a Balinese boy.

See bibliography for *Trance and Dance in Bali.*

Kypseli: Men and Women Apart (1974). Ca. 40 min. By Paul Aratow and Richard Cowan in collaboration with anthropologist Susannah Hoffman. Distributed by BM.

Closely follows Hoffman's ethnographic study of a Greek island community, emphasizing the many ways in which male and female roles are defined.

Latah (1983). 43 min. By Gunther Pfaff and Ronald Simons. Distributed by DER and ID.

Simons explores latah, the Malaysian hyperstartle syndrome, in a coastal village on the Malay Peninsula, with comparative footage from Japan and Michigan State University.

Simons, Ronald C. 1996. *Boo! Culture, experience, and the startle reflex.* New York: Oxford University Press.

Life Chances (1974). 43 min. By Peter Loizos. Distributed by RAI.

Among the Greek Cypriots, a man must provide a house for his daughter when she marries. The film follows two brothers, one who has several daughters and is still hoeing his fields in his old age, while the other, who has only sons, retires in comfort.

Loizos, Peter. 1975. *The Greek gift: Politics in a Cypriot village.* Oxford: Blackwell.

The Lion Hunters (1965). 68 min. Made by anthropologist Jean Rouch. Distributed by DER.

Shot on the upper Niger in West Africa, where farmers and pastoralists intermingle. Some villagers who are professional lion hunters are called in to kill lions that have been raiding the pastoralists' herd. But lion hunting is no casual matter, and the rituals of the hunt are shown in great detail.

Stoller, Paul. 1992. *The cinematic griot: The ethnography of Jean Rouch.* Chicago: University of Chicago Press.

Louisiana Story (1948). 77 min. By Robert Flaherty, with Richard Leacock as cameraman. Distributed by MOMA.

A lyrical picture of Cajun life in the Louisiana bayou country.

Calder-Marshall, Arthur. 1963. *The innocent eye: The life of Robert Flaherty.* London: W. H. Allen. See pp. 211–228.

Ma'bugi' Trance of the Toraja (1974). 30 min. Shot by anthropologist Eric Crystal and edited by Lee Rhoades. Distributed by PSU.

Follows the major trance ritual *(ma'bugi')* of a Toraja village in central Sulawesi (Celebes), Indonesia.

Les maîtres fous (1953). 30 min. By anthropologist Jean Rouch. Distributed by DER.

Tribesmen from the upper Niger who have come to Accra for work perform an annual Hauka ceremony, a violent trance performance in which they imitate (and mock) the British colonial government. The film first shows the men of the Hauka at their ordinary jobs, then follows the ceremony, and finally shows them again at their jobs the next day, explicitly suggesting that the cathartic blowout of the ceremony allows them to tolerate their daily drudgery.

Stoller, Paul. 1992. *The cinematic griot: The ethnography of Jean Rouch*. Chicago: University of Chicago Press.

Makiko's New World (1999). 57 min. By David Plath. Distributed by DER.

In 1910 a housewife in Kyoto, Japan, kept a diary of the ordinary events of her life. This film is a reenactment of the diary, using period photographs and actors.

Smith, Kazuko. 1995. *Makiko's diary*. Stanford, Calif.: Stanford University Press.

Margaret Mead's New Guinea Journal (1968). 90 min. By Craig Gilbert. Distributed by IU and PSU.

Shows Margaret Mead's 1968 return to Manus, where she had done ethnographic research in the 1920s, the 1950s, and the early 1960s. A rare view of an anthropologist in the field, the film also uses old photographs and footage to give an excellent history of Manus from the German colonial period through the Second World War, and from the postwar nativistic Paliau movement to the preparations for nationhood.

Mead, Margaret. 1930. *Growing up in New Guinea: A comparative study of primitive education*. New York: William Morrow and Co.
———. 1956. *New lives for old: Cultural transformation—Manus 1928–1953*. New York: William Morrow and Co.
Schwartz, Theodore. 1962. *The Paliau movement in the Admiralties, 1946–1954*. American Museum of Natural History Papers, vol. 49, pt. 2.

Maring in Motion: A Choreometric Analysis of Movement among a New Guinea People (1970?). 18 min. By Marek Jablonko in collaboration with anthropologist Alison Jablonko. Distributed by EMC.

A visual version of Alison Jablonko's unpublished ethnographic study of movement style—the first systematic application of Alan Lomax's choreometrics to a specific culture.

Matjemosh: A Woodcarver from the Village of Amanamkai—Asmat Tribe on the Southwest Coast of New Guinea (1970?). 27 min. By anthropologist Adriaan A. Gerbrands. Distributed by EMC.

Set on the Asmat coast of southern West New Guinea (now the Indonesian province of Irian Jaya). Focuses on the personality of Matjemosh, showing him in his cultural and social context, and follows his carving of a drum, going into the symbolic aspects of Asmat art.

Gerbrands, Adrian A. 1967. *Wow-ipits: Eight Asmat woodcarvers of New Guinea.* The Hague: Mouton.
Kiefer, Thomas M. 1966. Review of *Matjemosh. American Anthropologist* 68.1:300.

The Medium Is the Masseuse (1981). 30 min. By Timothy Asch, Patsy Asch, and Linda Connor. See *A Balinese Trance Séance.*

Microcultural Incidents in Ten Zoos (1971). 34 min. By J. D. Van Vlack in collaboration with anthropologist Ray L. Birdwhistell. Distributed by PSU.

A filmed version of a Birdwhistell lecture, illustrating the principles of kinesics. Uses footage from zoos in seven countries to show how people interact, communicate, and express themselves by nonverbal means when confronted with generally similar stimuli (mainly elephants).

Birdwhistell, Ray L. 1970. *Kinesics and context: Essays on body motion communication.* Philadelphia: University of Pennsylvania Press.

Moana: A Romance of the Golden Age (1926). 85 min. By Robert Flaherty. Distributed by MOMA.

Life and culture on Savaii, western Samoa. The highlight is the tattooing ceremony for the young man Moana.

Calder-Marshall, Arthur. 1963. *The innocent eye: The life of Robert Flaherty.* London: W. H. Allen. See pp. 98–120.

Mokil (1950). 58 min. By Conrad Bentzen.

A holistic picture of the Micronesian atoll of Mokil, showing the sorts of cultural and social changes that occur as a result of growing population and the shift from subsistence, cooperative economy to cash economy.

Kiste, Robert C., and Paul D. Schaefer. 1974. Review of *Mokil. American Anthropologist* 76.3:715–717.

The Moontrap (1963). 84 min. By Pierre Perrault, Michael Brault, and Marcel Carriere. Distributed by Cont/McG-H.

Set in a French-Canadian community on an island in the St. Lawrence River. Follows the efforts of the villagers to revive the catching of Beluga whales.

Mosori Monika (1970?). 20 min. By Chick Strand. Distributed by Cont/McG-H.
Shows the dilemma of the Warao Indians of Venezuela, caught between their own traditions and pressures to "modernize" and convert to Christianity. The narration speaks in the words of a Warao woman and a Spanish nun.

!Nai, the Story of a !Kung Woman (1980). 59 min. By John Marshall. Distributed by DER.
The life story of !Nai, using footage shot by John Marshall in the Kalahari over a period of thirty years.

See bibliography for *The Hunters*.

Nanook of the North (1922). 55 min. By Robert Flaherty. Distributed by MOMA and Cont/McG-H.
Vignettes from the life of the Eskimo hunter Nanook.

Calder-Marshall, Arthur. 1963. *The innocent eye: The life of Robert Flaherty*. London: W. H. Allen. See pp. 76–97.

Navajos Film Themselves Series (1966). Seven films made by Navajos as part of an experiment in semiotics of film, performed by Sol Worth and John Adair. Distributed by NYU.

Collier, John. 1974. Review of the series. *American Anthropologist* 76.2:481–486.
Worth, Sol, and John Adair. 1997. *Through Navajo eyes: An exploration in film communication and anthropology*. 2nd ed. Albuquerque: University of New Mexico Press.

Nawi (1971?). 22 min. By David and Judith MacDougall. Distributed by BM.
Shows the Jie cattle herders of Uganda as they prepare to go to their dry-season camps.

Gulliver, P. H. 1965. The Jie of Uganda. In *Peoples of Africa*, edited by James L. Gibbs Jr., pp. 157–196. New York: Holt, Rinehart, and Winston.

Neighborhood Tokyo (1992). 30 min. By Theodore Bestor. Distributed by DER.
Bestor's fieldwork in a Tokyo neighborhood.

Bestor, Theodore C. 1989. *Neighborhood Tokyo*. Stanford, Calif.: Stanford University Press.

Netsilik Eskimo Series (1967–1968). Some dozen films, produced by the Educational Development Corporation in collaboration with anthropologists Asen Balikci and Guy Mary-Rousseliere. Distributed by UEVA.

Reconstructed technology of the Netsilik Eskimos of Pelly Bay (Canada). The films were prepared for secondary school educational packages.

Balikci, Asen, and Quentin Brown. 1966. Ethnographic filming and the Netsilik Eskimos. In *Educational Services Incorporated quarterly report, spring–summer 1966*, pp. 19–33. Newton, Mass.: Educational Services Inc.

No Longer Strangers (1966?). Ca. 25 min.

A missionary account of the conversion of the Western Dani of Irian Jaya, Indonesia. (The Western Dani live just to the west of the Grand Valley Dani of *Dead Birds*.)

O'Brien, Denise, and Anton Ploeg. 1964. Acculturation movements among the Western Dani. *American Anthropologist* 66.4.2:281–292.

The Nuer (1970). 73 min. By Hilary Harris and George Breidenbach, with the assistance of Robert Gardner. Distributed by DER.

A poetic film concentrating on evocative images of life among a group of Nuer living in Ethiopia. Creates a strong and memorable impression of the people, their cattle, their artifacts, and their land. On occasion, an English narration is used to give a more ethnographic account of events, especially a bride-price dispute; a ghost marriage; a revitalistic ceremony intended to combat a smallpox epidemic; and the climax of the film, a *gar* initiation, where two boys receive the forehead incisions of manhood.

Beidelman, T. O. 1966. The ox and Nuer sacrifice. *Man* 1:453–467.
———. 1968. Some Nuer notions of nakedness, nudity, and sexuality. *Africa* 38: 113–131.
Evans-Pritchard, E. E. 1940. *The Nuer: A description of the modes of livelihood and political institutions of a Nilotic people.* Oxford: Oxford University Press.

Number Our Days (1983). 29 min. By Lynne Littman, with Barbara Myerhoff. Distributed by Direct Cinema.

Retired Jewish immigrants in a home in Venice, California. Academy Award for Best Documentary, Short Subject, 1977.

Myerhoff, Barbara. 1979. *"Number our days": Culture and community among elderly Jews in an American ghetto.* New York: Meridian.

N/um Tchai: The Ceremonial Dance of the !Kung Bushmen (1966). 25 min. By John Marshall. Distributed by DER.

The curing ritual of the Kalahari Bushmen, in which the curers go into trance.

Lee, Richard B. 1968. The sociology of !Kung Bushman trance performances. In *Trance and possession states,* edited by Raymond H. Prince, pp. 35–54. Montreal: R. M. Bucke Memorial Society.

Marshall, Lorna. 1969. The medicine dance of the !Kung Bushmen. *Africa* 39.4:381–437.

Palm Play (1980). 29 min. By Alan Lomax, with Forrestine Paulay. Distributed by EMC.

Film clips illustrating the various positions of hands in dance and play, following Lomax's choreometrics system.

The Path (1972). 34 min. By Donald Rundstrom, Ronald Rundstrom, and Clinton Bergum.

Depicts the Japanese tea ceremony, using the aesthetics of the *d\o,* or "the way," to shape the structure of the film. It is about balance and energy.

Rundstrom, Donald, Ronald Rundstrom, and Clinton Bergum. 1973. *Japanese tea: The ritual, the aesthetics, the way; An ethnographic companion to the film "The path."* New York: MSS Information Corp.

People of the Australian Western Desert (1969). A ten-part series of films made by Ian Dunlop for the Australian Institute of Aboriginal Studies, in collaboration with anthropologist Robert Tonkinson. Distributed by PSU and RAI.

The series concentrates on the subsistence technology of the Aborigines of the Western Desert of Australia. The films were shot of a family that had been living at a mission station but agreed to return to the desert with the film crew.

Tonkinson, Robert. 1974. *The Jigalong mob: Aboriginal victors of the desert crusade.* Menlo Park, Calif.: Cummings.

Pomo Shaman (1964). 20 min. (abridged version of *Sucking Doctor,* which is 45 minutes long). See *The American Indian Series.*

Shows the highlights of a curing ceremony performed by Essie Parrish, the last shaman of the Kashia (southwestern) Pomo Indians of California.

Primates Like Us (2003). 20 min. By Devi Shively, with Agustin Fuentes. Distributed by BM.

Fuentes leads an undergraduate research project studying macaques in Ubud, Bali.

Ramparts of Clay (1969). Ca. 60 min. Distributed by C5.

A fictionalized account of life in the Tunisian village that had been described in Duvignaud's ethnography. The film itself was shot in Algeria.

Duvignaud, Jean. 1970. *Change at Shebika: Report from a North African village.* Translated from the French by Frances Frenaye. New York: Pantheon Books.

Releasing the Spirits: A Village Cremation in Bali (1991). 43 min. By Timothy Asch, Patsy Asch, and Linda Connor. Distributed by DER.

The fifth film in the Jero Tapakan series. A Balinese village sponsors a great cremation ceremony for all those who have died in the recent past. See *A Balinese Trance Séance.*

Rivers of Sand (1974). 85 min. By Robert Gardner. Distributed by DER.

This film about the Hamar cattle herders of southwestern Ethiopia emphasizes the life of women and their role in the Hamar society by returning again and again to one Hamar woman who describes her life.

Song of Ceylon (1934). 45 min. Made by Basil Wright and John Grierson for the Ceylon Tea Propaganda Board. Distributed by MOMA.

A series of images showing various views of Ceylon and the Buddhist aspects of the culture.

Step Style (1980). 29 min. By Alam Lomax, with Forrestine Paulay. Distributed by EMC.

Film clips showing the various ways of stepping according to the Lomax choreometrics system.

Tidikawa and Friends (1973). Ca. 80 min. By Jeff and Su Doring.

Evokes a mood of events in the life of the Bedamini of Papua New Guinea.

Schieffelin, Edward L., and Bambi B. Schieffelin. 1974. Review of *Tidikawa and friends. American Anthropologist* 76.3:710–714.

Timing Death (2000). 52 min. By Kathrin Oester. (Indonesian title: *Sulang-Sulang;* German title: *Der Abschied.*) Distributed by Artefakt Productions.

Among the Batak of North Sumatra, Indonesia, the community performs the *sulang-sulang* ceremony, a sort of pre-funeral, when a person is near death.

To Find Our Life: The Peyote Hunt of the Huichols of Mexico (1968). 65 min. By anthropologist Peter T. Furst. Distributed by PSU.

Follows a group of Huichols on their ritual quest for the sacred peyote.

Furst, Peter T. 1972. *To find our life: Peyote among the Huichol Indians of Mexico.* In *Flesh of the gods: The ritual use of hallucinogens,* edited by Peter T. Furst, pp. 136–184. New York: Praeger.

La Barre, Weston. 1970. Review of *To find our life. American Anthropologist* 72:1201.

Myerhoff, Barbara G. 1974. *Peyote hunt: The sacred journey of the Huichol Indians.* Ithaca, N.Y.: Cornell University Press.

Trance and Dance in Bali (1952). 20 min. By Gregory Bateson and Margaret Mead. Distributed by NYU.

A ritual performance filmed in Bali about 1938. The two protagonists, the witch and the dragon, struggle over good and evil, life and death. Many people go into deep trance, and men turn their swords against themselves.

Bateson, Gregory, and Margaret Mead. 1942. *Balinese character: A photographic analysis.* Special Publications of the New York Academy of Sciences, vol. 2. New York.
Belo, Jane. 1960. *Trance in Bali.* New York: Columbia University Press.
————, ed. 1970. *Traditional Balinese culture.* New York: Columbia University Press.

Trobriand Cricket (1976). 54 min. By Gary Kildea, with Jerry Leach. Distributed by BM.

Sixty years after Bronislaw Malinowski did his famous fieldwork on the Trobriand Islands, east of New Guinea, this film shows how the Trobrianders accepted and altered the British game of cricket to fit their own culture.

Leach, Jerry W. 1988. Structure and message in *Trobriand cricket.* In *Anthropological film-making,* edited by Jack R. Rollwagon, pp. 237–251. Chur, Switzerland: Harwood Academic Publishers.

The Turtle People (1973). 26 min. Shot by anthropologist Brian Weiss and edited by James Ward.

Made as a visual report of Weiss's ecological ethnographic study of the Miskito Indians of Nicaragua. Explains how the Miskito, who have ridden one economic boom after another and always emerged poorer than before, are now depleting their sea turtle population, their best source of protein, to sell to a canning company.

Gross, Daniel R. 1974. Review of *The Turtle People. American Anthropologist* 76 : 486 – 487.

The Village (1969). 70 min. By Mark McCarty in collaboration with anthropologist Paul Hockings. Distributed by DER.

Impressions and scenes of the village of Dunquin, County Kerry, Ireland, emphasizing the problems of modernization.

We Believe in Niño Fidencio (1973). Ca. 40 min. By anthropologists Jon Olson and Natalie Olson.

An account of a pilgrimage center in northern Mexico—a Catholic cult of the Niño Fidencio, who performed healing acts. Told from the viewpoint of the believers.

Wedding of Palo (1937). 72 min. By Friedrich Dalsheim in collaboration with anthropologist Knud Rasmussen. Distributed by MOMA.

Written by Danish-Eskimo anthropologist Knud Rasmussen and acted by Eskimos on location in eastern Greenland. Apparently a traditional Eskimo love story. Uses fiction to explore the important aspects of Eskimo emotions and culture.

Yanomamö: A Multi-disciplinary Study (1971?). 45 min. By Timothy Asch in collaboration with anthropologist Napoleon Chagnon and geneticist James V. Neel. Distributed by DER.

An account of a medical research expedition to study the Yanomamö Indians of southern Venezuela, with much general ethnographic background.

See bibliography for *The Feast.*

BIBLIOGRAPHY

Anderson, Carolyn, and Thomas W. Benson

1988   Direct cinema and the myth of informed consent: The case of *Titicut Follies*. In *Image ethics: The moral rights of subjects in photographs, film, and television,* edited by Larry Gross, John Stuart Katz, and Jay Ruby, pp. 58–90. New York: Oxford University Press.

Arruda, Suzanne Middendorf

2001   *From Kansas to cannibals: The story of Osa Johnson.* Greensboro, N.C.: Avisson Press.

Asch, Timothy

1972   Ethnographic filming and the Yanomamö Indians. *Sightlines* 5.3:6–17.

1974   Audiovisual materials in the teaching of anthropology from elementary school through college. In *Education and cultural process: Toward an anthropology of education,* edited by George D. Spindler, pp. 463–490. New York: Holt, Rinehart, and Winston.

Balikci, Asen, and Quentin Brown

1966   Ethnographic filming and the Netsilik Eskimos. In *Educational Services Incorporated quarterly report, spring–summer 1966,* pp. 19–33. Newton, Mass.: Educational Services Inc.

Banks, Marcus, and Howard Morphy, eds.

1997   *Rethinking visual anthropology.* New Haven, Conn.: Yale University Press.

Barbash, Ilisa, and Lucien Taylor

1997   *Cross-cultural filmmaking: A handbook for making documentary and ethnographic films and videos.* Berkeley: University of California Press.

Barrett, S. A.

1961   American Indian films. *Kroeber Anthropological Society Papers* 25:155–162.

Barsam, R. M.

1988   *The vision of Robert Flaherty: The artist as myth and filmmaker.* Bloomington: Indiana University Press.

Barth, Fredrik

1961   *Nomads of South Persia: The Basseri tribe of the Khamseh Confederacy.* Boston: Little, Brown, and Co.

Bateson, Gregory

1939   *Naven: A survey of the problems suggested by a composite picture of the culture of a New Guinea tribe drawn from three points of view.* 2nd ed. Stanford, Calif.: Stanford University Press, 1958.

1949   Bali: The value system of a steady state. In *Social Structure: Studies Presented to A. R. Radcliffe-Brown,* edited by Meyer Fortes, pp. 35–53. New York: Russell and Russell.

1972   *Steps to an ecology of mind.* New York: Ballantine Books. (Orig. pub. 1960.)

Bateson, Gregory, and Margaret Mead

1942   *Balinese character: A photographic analysis.* Special Publications of the New York Academy of Sciences, vol. 2. New York.

Behlmer, Rudy

1966   Merian C. Cooper. *Films in Review* 17.1:17–35.

Benedict, Ruth

1934   *Patterns of culture.* New York: Houghton Mifflin.

Bestor, Theodore C.

1989   *Neighborhood Tokyo.* Stanford, Calif.: Stanford University Press.

Biella, Peter, Gary Seaman, and Napoleon Chagnon

1997   *Yanomamo interactive: Understanding "The ax fight."* Fort Worth: Harcourt Brace. CD-ROM.

Birdwhistell, Ray L.

1963   The use of audio-visual teaching aids. In *Resources for the teaching of anthropology,* American Anthropological Association Memoir 95, edited by David G. Mandelbaum, Gabriel W. Lasker, and Ethel M. Albert. Berkeley: University of California Press.

1970   *Kinesics and context: Essays on body motion communication.* Philadelphia: University of Pennsylvania Press.

Bishop, John

2001–2002   Alan Lomax 1915–2002: A remembrance; Alan Lomax and visual anthropology. *Visual Anthropology Review* 17.2:13–23.

Broekhuijse, J. Th.

1967   *De Wiligiman-Dani: Een cultureel-anthropologische studie over religie en oorlogvoering in de Baliem-vallei.* Tilburg: H. Gianotten N.V.

Calder-Marshall, Arthur

1963   *The innocent eye: The life of Robert Flaherty.* London: W. H. Allen.

Cancian, Frank

1965   *Economics and prestige in a Maya community.* Stanford, Calif.: Stanford University Press.

Carpenter, Edmund
1972   *Oh, what a blow that phantom gave me!* New York: Holt, Rinehart, and Winston.

Chagnon, Napoleon
1997   *Yanomamö: The fierce people.* 5th ed. Fort Worth: Harcourt Brace.

Chalfen, Richard
1997   New introduction, afterword, and notes to *Through Navajo eyes,* edited by Sol Worth and John Adair. Albuquerque: University of New Mexico Press.

Chapple, Eliot Dismore, and Carleton Stevens Coon
1942   *Principles of anthropology.* New York: Henry Holt and Co.

Chiozzi, Paolo, and Franz Haller, eds.
1988   *Issues in visual anthropology.* Aachen: Alano Verlag.

Cole, Catherine M.
2001   *Ghana's concert party theatre.* Bloomington: Indiana University Press.

Condon, W. S., and W. D. Ogston
1966   Sound film analysis of normal and pathological behavior patterns. *Journal of Nervous and Mental Disorders* 143:338–347.

Conklin, Harold
1957   *Hanunóo agriculture: A report on an integral system of shifting cultivation in the Philippines.* Rome: Food and Agriculture Organization of the United Nations.

Connor, Linda, Patsy Asch, and Timothy Asch
1986   *Jero Tapakan, Balinese healer: An ethnographic film monograph.* Cambridge: Cambridge University Press. Rev. ed., Los Angeles: Ethnographic Press, Center for Visual Anthropology, University of Southern California, 1996.

Cooper, Merian C.
1925   *Grass.* New York: G. P. Putnam's Sons.

Cooper, Thomas W.
1995   *Natural rhythms: The indigenous world of Robert Gardner.* New York: Anthology Film Archives.

Crawford, Peter Jan, and David Turton, eds.
1992   *Film as ethnography.* Manchester: Manchester University Press.

Danzker, Jo-Anne Birnie
1980   Robert Flaherty/photographer. *Studies in Visual Communication* 6.2:5–32.

Davis, Martha
2001–2002   Film projectors as microscopes: Ray L. Birdwhistell and microanalysis of interaction (1955–1975). *Visual Anthropology Review* 17.2:39–49.

Devereaux, Leslie, and Roger Hillman, eds.
1995   *Fields of vision: Essays in film studies, visual anthropology, and photography.* Berkeley: University of California Press.

Duvignaud, Jean
1970   *Change at Shebika: Report from a North African village.* Translated from the French by Frances Frenaye. New York: Pantheon Books.

Ekman, P., and W. V. Friesen
1969a   Nonverbal leakage and clues to deception. *Psychiatry* 32.1:88–106.
1969b   The repertoire of nonverbal behavior: Categories, origins, usage, and coding. *Semiotica* 1.1:49–98.

Elder, Sarah
2001–2002   Images of Asch. *Visual Anthropology Review* 17.2:89–109.

El Guindi, Fadwa
1996   *El Sebou': Film study guide.* Egyptian Celebration of Life Series. Los Angeles: El Nil Foundation.
2004   *Visual anthropology: Essential method and theory.* Walnut Creek, Calif.: AltaMira.

Evans-Pritchard, E. E.
1940   *The Nuer: A description of the modes of livelihood and political institutions of a Nilotic people.* Oxford: Oxford University Press.

Feld, Steve
1974   Avant propos: Jean Rouch. *Studies in the Anthropology of Visual Communication* 1.1:35–36.

Fischer, David Hackett
1970   *Historians' fallacies: Toward a logic of historical thought.* New York: Harper and Row.

Gardner, Robert
1990   The more things change. *Transition* 58:34–66.
2006   *The impulse to preserve: Reflections of a filmmaker.* New York: Other Press.

Gardner, Robert, and Karl G. Heider
1969   *Gardens of war: Life and death in the New Guinea Stone Age.* New York: Random House.

Gardner, Robert, and Ákos Östör
1989   Die Einfache Ringelblume: Robert Gardner und Ákos Östör sprechen ueber *Forest of Bliss.* In *Rituale von Leben und Tod: Robert Gardner und seine filme,* edited by R. Kapfer, W. Petermann, and R. Thoms, pp. 102–128. Munich: Trickster.
2001   *Making "Forest of bliss": Intention, circumstance, and chance in nonfiction film.* Cambridge, Mass.: Harvard University Press.
2004 [1964] *Dead birds.* Cambridge, Mass: Film Study Center of the Peabody Museum at Harvard University. DVD.

Gerbrands, Adrian A.
1967   *Wow-ipits: Eight Asmat woodcarvers of New Guinea.* The Hague: Mouton.

Griffith, Richard

1953   *The world of Robert Flaherty.* New York: Duell, Sloan, and Pearce.

Griffiths, Alison

2002   *Wondrous difference: Cinema, anthropology, and turn-of-the-century visual culture.* New York: Columbia University Press.

Grimshaw, Anna

2001   *The ethnographers' eye: Ways of seeing in modern anthropology.* Cambridge: Cambridge University Press.

Grimshaw, Anna, and Amanda Ravetz, eds.

2005   *Visualizing anthropology.* Bristol, UK: Intellect.

Gross, Larry, John Stuart Katz, and Jay Ruby, eds.

1988   *Image ethics: The moral rights of subjects in photographs, film, and television.* New York: Oxford University Press.

Halberstadt, Ira

1974   An interview with Fred Wiseman. *Filmmakers Newsletter* 7.4:19–25.

Harris, Marvin

1979   *Cows, pigs, wars, and witches: The riddles of culture.* New York: Random House.

Hart, David M.

2001   *Muslim tribesmen and the colonial encounter in fiction and on film.* Amsterdam: Het Spinhuis.

Heider, John

1974   Catharsis in human potential encounter. *Journal of Humanist Psychology* 14.4:27–47.

Heider, Karl G.

1969   Attributes and categories in the study of material culture: New Guinea Dani attire. *Man* 4.3:379–391.

1970   *The Dugum Dani: A Papuan culture in the highlands of West New Guinea.* Chicago: Aldine.

1972a   *The Dani of West Irian: An ethnographic companion to the film "Dead birds."* New York: MSS Information Corp.

1972b   The Grand Valley Dani pig feast: A ritual of passage and intensification. *Oceania* 42.3:169–197.

1974a   The attributes of ethnographic film. *Newsletter of the Society for the Anthropology of Visual Communication* 5.2:4–6.

1974b   *Ethnographic films: Lifelong learning.* 44.21:1–5. Berkeley: University of California Extension Media Center.

1977   From Javanese to Dani: The translation of a game. In *Studies in the anthropology of play,* edited by Phillips Stevens Jr., pp. 72–80. West Point, N.Y.: Leisure Press.

1988 The Rashomon effect: When ethnographers disagree. *American Anthropologist* 90.1:73–81.

1991a *Indonesian cinema: National culture on screen.* Honolulu: University of Hawaii Press.

1991b *Landscapes of emotion: Mapping three cultures of emotion in Indonesia.* Cambridge: Cambridge University Press.

1997a *Grand Valley Dani: Peaceful warriors.* 3rd ed. Fort Worth: Harcourt Brace.

1997b *Seeing anthropology: Cultural anthropology through film.* Boston: Allyn and Bacon.

2001–2002 Robert Gardner: The early years. *Visual Anthropology Review* 17.2:61–70.

2004a An 18-minute trip to the field. In *Strategies in teaching anthropology,* 3rd ed., edited by Patricia C. Rice and David W. McCurdy, pp. 131–134. Upper Saddle River, N.J.: Prentice Hall.

2004b *Seeing anthropology: Cultural anthropology through film.* 3rd ed. Boston: Allyn and Bacon.

2005 Gardner's first shots: Vectored landscapes. Paper presented at the annual meeting of the American Anthropological Association, Washington, D.C., 1 December.

Heider, Karl G., and Carol Hermer

1995 *Films for anthropological teaching.* 8th ed. Arlington, Va.: American Anthropological Association.

Henley, Paul

2005 Review of *Timothy Asch and Ethnographic Film,* edited by E. D. Lewis. *Journal of the Royal Anthropological Institute* 11.1:151–152.

Himpele, Jeff, ed.

2004 Gaining ground: Indigenous video in Bolivia, Mexico, and beyond. *American Anthropologist* 106.2:353–373.

Himpele, Jeff, and Faye Ginsburg, eds.

2005 Ciné-trance: A tribute to Jean Rouch (1917–2004). *American Anthropologist* 107.1:108–129.

Hockings, Paul

2001–2002 Asen Balikci films Nanook. *Visual Anthropology Review* 17.2:71–80.

Hockings, Paul, ed.

1995 *Principles of visual anthropology.* 2nd ed. Berlin: Mouton de Gruyter.

Husman, Rolf, Ingrid Wellinger, Johannes Ruehl, and Martin Taureg

1992 *A bibliography of ethnographic film.* Göttingen: LIT Verlag.

Imperato, Pascal James, and Eleanor M. Imperato

1992 *They married adventure: The wandering lives of Martin and Osa Johnson.* New Brunswick, N.J.: Rutgers University Press.

Jablonko, Alison

2001–2002   An intersection of disciplines: The development of choreometrics in the
             1960s. *Visual Anthropology Review* 17.2:24–38.

Jacknis, Ira

1984   Franz Boas and photography. *Studies in Visual Communication* 10.1:2–60.

Johnson, Osa

1940   *I married adventure: The lives and adventures of Martin and Osa Johnson.*
             Philadelphia: J. B. Lippincott.

Kapfer, R., W. Petermann, and R. Thoms, eds.

1989   *Rituale von Leben und Tod: Robert Gardner und seine filme.* Munich:
             Trickster.

Kaplan, Daile

1984   Enlightened women in darkened lands—A lantern slide lecture. *Studies in
             Visual Communication* 10.1:61–77.

Kendon, Adam, and Andrew Ferber

1973   A description of some human greetings. In *Comparative ecology and be-
             havior of primates,* edited by R. P. Michael and J. H. Crook, pp. 591–668.
             London: Academic Press.

Lansing, J. Stephen

1991   *Priests and programmers: Technologies of power in the engineered landscape of
             Bali.* Princeton, N.J.: Princeton University Press.

1995   *The Balinese.* Fort Worth: Harcourt Brace College Publishers.

Larson, Erik

2003   *The devil in the White City: Murder, magic, and madness at the fair that
             changed America.* New York: Vintage Books.

Lee, Richard B.

2002   *The Dobe Ju/'hoansi.* 3rd ed. Fort Worth: Harcourt Brace.

Lee, Richard B., and Irven De Vore

1968   *Man the hunter.* Chicago: Aldine.

Lévi-Strauss, Claude

1955   *Tristes tropiques.* English translation by John and Doreen Weightman; New
             York: Atheneum, 1974.

Lewis, E. D., ed.

2004   *Timothy Asch and ethnographic film.* London: Routledge.

Lindstrom, Lamont

Forthcoming They sold adventure: Martin and Osa Johnson in the New Hebrides. In
             *Tarzan was an ecotourist, and other reflections in the anthropology of ad-
             venture,* edited by Luis A. Vivanco and Robert A. Gordon. New York:
             Berghahn Books.

Loizos, Peter
1975   *The Greek gift: Politics in a Cypriot village.* Oxford: Blackwell.
1993   *Innovation in ethnographic film: From innocence to self-consciousness, 1955–1985.* Chicago: University of Chicago Press.

Lomax, Alan
1973   Cinema, science, and cultural renewal. *Current Anthropology* 14.4:474–480.

Loud, Pat, with Nora Johnson
1974   *Pat Loud: A woman's story.* New York: Coward, McCann, and Geoghegan.

MacDougall, David
1998   *Transcultural cinema.* Princeton, N.J.: Princeton University Press.
2001a   Renewing ethnographic film: Is digital video changing the genre? *Anthropology Today* 17.3:15–21.
2001b   Review of *Making "Forest of bliss,"* by Robert Gardner and Ákos Östör. *Visual Anthropology Review* 17.1:1–18.

Malinowski, Bronislaw
1922   *Argonauts of the Western Pacific.* New York: E. P. Dutton.
1923   The problem of meaning in primitive languages. In *The meaning of meaning,* edited by C. K. Ogden and I. A. Richards, pp. 296–336. New York: Harcourt, Brace, and World.
1929   *The sexual life of savages in north-western Melanesia.* New York: Harcourt, Brace, and World.

Marshall, John
1958   Man as a hunter. *Natural History* 67.6:291–309; 67.7:376–395.

Marshall, John, and John W. Adams
1978   Jean Rouch talks about his films to John Marshall and John W. Adams. *American Anthropologist* 80.4:1005–1022. Reprinted in *Ciné-ethnography,* by Jean Rouch, edited and translated by Steven Feld, pp. 188–209; Minneapolis: University of Minnesota Press, 2003.

Marshall, Lorna
1957   The kin terminology system of the !Kung Bushmen. *Africa* 27.1:1–25.

Marshall, Lorna, and Megan Biesele
1974   *N/um Tchai: The ceremonial dance of the !Kung Bushmen: A study guide.* Somerville, Mass.: Documentary Educational Resources.

Matthiessen, Peter
1962   *Under the mountain wall: A chronicle of two seasons in the Stone Age.* New York: Viking.

Mauss, Marcel
1925   *The gift: Forms and functions of exchange in archaic societies.* English translation by Ian Cunnison; London: Cohen and West, 1954.

Maybury-Lewis, David
1967   *Akwe-Shavante society.* Oxford: Clarendon Press.

Mead, Margaret
1928   *Coming of age in Samoa.* New York: William Morrow and Co.
1930a   *Growing up in New Guinea: A comparative study of primitive education.* New York: William Morrow and Co.
1930b   *Social organization of Manua.* Bishop Museum Bulletin, no. 76. Honolulu.
1935   *Sex and temperament in three primitive societies.* New York: William Morrow and Co.
1970   The art and technology of field work. In *A handbook of method in cultural anthropology,* edited by Raoul Naroll and Ronald Cohen, pp. 246–265. Garden City, N.Y.: Natural History Press.
1972   *Blackberry winter: My earlier years.* New York: William Morrow and Co.

Mead, Margaret, and Frances Cook MacGregor
1951   *Growth and culture: A photographic study of Balinese childhood.* New York: G. P. Putnam's Sons.

Meiselas, Susan
2003   *Encounters with the Dani: Stories from the Baliem Valley.* Göttingen: Steidl.

Metz, Christian
1974   *Film language: A semiotics of the cinema.* New York: Oxford University Press.

Morris, Rosalind C.
1994   *New worlds from fragments: Film, ethnography, and the representation of Northwest Coast cultures.* Boulder, Colo.: Westview.

Mugge, Robert
1974   Film grants. *Filmmakers Newsletter* 7.7:52–57; 7.8:78–82.

Mullen, Pat
1935   *Man of Aran.* New York: E. P. Dutton.

Murdock, George Peter
1972   Anthropology's mythology. In *Proceedings of the Royal Anthropological Institute of Great Britain and Ireland for 1971,* pp. 17–24. London.

Ndambuki, Berida, and Claire C. Robertson
2000   *We only come here to struggle: Stories from Berida's life.* Bloomington: Indiana University Press.

Oliver, Douglas L.
1955   *A Solomon Island society.* Cambridge, Mass.: Harvard University Press.

O'Reilly, Patrick
1970   Le "documentaire" ethnographique en Océanie. In *Premier catalogue sélectif international de films ethnographiques sur la région du Pacifique,* pp. 281–305. Paris: UNESCO.

Östör, Ákos
1994   *Forest of Bliss:* Film and anthropology. *East-West Film Journal* 8.2:70–104.

Papademas, Diana, ed.
2004   Ethics in visual research. Special issue, *Visual Studies* 19.2.

Pincus, Edward
1969   *Guide to filmmaking.* New York: New American Library.

Pink, Sarah
2001   *Doing visual ethnography: Images, media, and representation in research.* London: Sage.

Pink, Sarah, Laszlo Kurti, and Ana Isabel Afonso, eds.
2004   *Working images: Visual research and representation in ethnography.* London: Routledge.

Prins, Harald E. L.
1992   Bwana Piccer: Martin Johnson as ethnographic film pioneer. Invited paper presented at the 91st annual meeting of the American Anthropological Association, San Francisco, 12 December.

Radcliffe-Brown, A. R.
1922   *The Andaman Islanders.* Cambridge: Cambridge University Press.

Raymond, Alan, and Susan Raymond
1973   Filming an American family. *Filmmakers Newsletter* 6.5:19–21.

Read, Kenneth E.
1965   *The high valley.* New York: Charles Scribner's Sons.

Reichlin, Seth
1974a   *"Baobab play": Film notes.* Somerville, Mass: Documentary Educational Resources.

1974b   *"Bitter melons": A study guide.* Somerville, Mass.: Documentary Educational Resources.

1974c   *"Children throw toy assegais": Film notes.* Somerville, Mass.: Documentary Educational Resources.

1974d   *"The lion game": Film notes.* Somerville, Mass: Documentary Educational Resources.

1974e   *"The meat fight": A study guide.* Somerville, Mass.: Documentary Education Resources.

1974f   *"Tug of war": Film notes.* Somerville, Mass: Documentary Educational Resources.

1974g   *"The wasp nest": A study guide.* Somerville, Mass.: Documentary Education Resources.

Reichlin, Seth, and John Marshall
1974   *"An argument about a marriage": The study guide.* Somerville, Mass: Documentary Educational Resources.

Rony, Fatimah Tobing
1996   *The third eye: Race, cinema, and ethnographic spectacle.* Durham, N.C.:
            Duke University Press.

Rotha, Paul
1983   *Robert Flaherty: A biography.* Edited by Jay Ruby. Philadelphia: University
            of Pennsylvania Press.

Rotha, Paul, and Basil Wright
1980   Nanook and the north. *Studies in Visual Communication* 6.2:33–60.

Rouch, Jean
1956   Migrations au Ghana, Gold Coast, enquêtes 1953–1955. *Journal de la So-
            ciété des Africanistes* 26.1–2:33–196.
1970   Avant propos. In *Premier catalogue sélectif international de films ethno-
            graphiques sur la région du Pacifique,* pp 13–20. Paris: UNESCO.
1974   The camera and man. *Studies in the Anthropology of Visual Communication*
            1.1:37–144.
2003   *Ciné-ethnography.* Edited and translated by Steven Feld. Minneapolis:
            University of Minnesota Press.

Ruby, Jay
2000   *Picturing culture: Explorations of film and anthropology.* Chicago: University
            of Chicago Press.

Ruby, Jay, ed.
1993   *The cinema of John Marshall.* Chur, Switzerland: Harwood Academic
            Publishers.

Rundstrom, Donald, Ronald Rundstrom, and Clinton Bergum
1973   *Japanese tea: The ritual, the aesthetics, the way; An ethnographic companion
            to the film "The path."* New York: MSS Information Corp.

Russell, Catherine
1999   *Experimental ethnography: The work of film in the age of video.* Durham,
            N.C.: Duke University Press.

Scheflen, Albert E.
1973   *Communicational structure: Analysis of a psychotherapy transaction.* Bloom-
            ington: Indiana University Press.

Shaheen, Jack G.
1988   Perspectives on the television Arab. In *Image ethics,* edited by Larry Gross,
            John Stuart Katz, and Jay Ruby, pp. 203–219. New York: Oxford Univer-
            sity Press.
2001   *Reel bad Arabs: How Hollywood vilifies a people.* New York: Olive Branch
            Press.

Skinner, Eliott P., ed.
1972   *Peoples and cultures of Africa.* New York: Natural History Press.

Smith, Kazuko
1995   *Makiko's diary.* Stanford, Calif.: Stanford University Press.

Sorenson, E. Richard
1967   A research film program in the study of changing man. *Current Anthropology* 8.5:443–460.

1974   Anthropological film: A scientific and humanistic resource. *Science* 186. 4169:1079–1085.

Stoller, Paul
1992   *The cinematic griot: The ethnography of Jean Rouch.* Chicago: University of Chicago Press.

1999   *Jaguar: A story of Africans in America.* Chicago: University of Chicago Press.

Stott, Kenhelm W., Jr.
1978   *Exploring with Martin and Osa Johnson.* Chanute, Kans.: Martin and Osa Johnson Safari Museum.

Taylor, Lucien
2002   A life on the edge of film and anthropology. In *Ciné-ethnography,* by Jean Rouch, edited and translated by Steven Feld, pp. 128–146. Minneapolis: University of Minnesota Press.

Taylor, Lucien, ed.
1994   *Visualizing theory: Selected essays from VAR, 1990–1994.* New York: Routledge.

Thomas, Elizabeth Marshall
1959   *The harmless people.* New York: Knopf.

Tonkinson, Robert
1974   *The Jigalong mob: Aboriginal victors of the desert crusade.* Menlo Park, Calif.: Cummings.

Turner, Terrence
1991   The social dynamics of video media in an Indigenous society: The cultural meaning and personal politics of video-making in Kayapo communities. *Visual Anthropology Review* 7.2:68–72.

Volkman, Toby Alice
1988   Out of South Africa: *The gods must be crazy.* In *Image ethics,* edited by Stuart Katz and Jay Ruby, pp. 236–247. New York: Oxford University Press.

Wood, Robin
1971   *The Apu trilogy.* New York: Praeger.

Worth, Sol
1969   The development of a semiotic of film. *Semiotica* 1.3: 282–321.

Worth, Sol, and John Adair
1972   *Through Navajo eyes: An exploration in film communication and anthropology.* Bloomington: Indiana University Press. 2nd ed.; Albuquerque: University of New Mexico Press, 1997.

INDEX